The Thinking Workshop

Creativity, Bias, and the Architecture of Reason

Mark Donnelly, PhD.

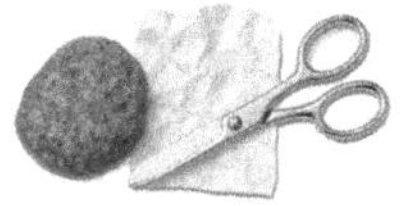

RPSS PUBLISHING - BUFFALO, NEW YORK

drmaddog@hotmail.com

The Thinking Workshop

Perfect Bound ISBN:978-1-956688-74-0

Printed in the United States of America

10 9 8 7 6 5 4 3 2 1

RPSS Publishing - Buffalo, New York

Ideas are born with enthusiasm,

raised by assumption,

and eventually judged by structure.

Miss any one of those steps,

and you don't have thinking.

You have a well-dressed guess.

Table of Contents

Introduction

The Workshop Behind Your Forehead

There is a certain comforting myth we all carry around like a well-worn coat: that we are, at our core, rational creatures. We imagine ourselves as careful thinkers, weighing evidence, considering alternatives, arriving, after due deliberation, at sensible conclusions.

This is a flattering story.

It is also, on most days, fiction.

What we actually do is something far less orderly and far more interesting. We reach conclusions quickly, often invisibly, and then–like a homeowner explaining a house that appeared overnight–we construct reasons to justify what is already standing.

The mind, it turns out, is not a courtroom.

It is a workshop.

And not the pristine kind you see in catalogs, where every wrench hangs at a perfect angle and the floor is clean enough to eat off. No, this is the workshop behind the hardware store. A little cluttered. A little noisy. Full of useful tools and questionable decisions. Something is always being built. Something else is always being repaired. And occasionally, something is quietly falling apart in the corner while no one is looking.

If you listen carefully, you'll notice the place is not empty. Three regulars are always at work.

The first is the Inventor

This one is enthusiastic. Tireless. A collector of half-formed ideas and unlikely connections. The Inventor sees patterns where none exist and possibilities where none were requested. Give this character a problem, and you will not get one solution. You will get twelve, two of which are brilliant, six of which are impractical, and four of which should never be spoken aloud in a professional setting.

The second is the Shortcutter

Efficient to a fault. Impatient. The Shortcutter dislikes uncertainty the way some people dislike long lines at the grocery store. It reaches for the nearest explanation, the most familiar pattern, the easiest answer. It fills in gaps, smooths over complexity, and assures you–quietly but confidently–that you already know enough. It is the reason you can recognize a face in a crowd in a fraction of a second. It is also the reason you sometimes mistake confidence for correctness.

The third is the Inspector

Less popular. Slower. Frequently ignored. The Inspector asks inconvenient questions. "How do you know?" "What's the evidence?" "Does that actually follow?" It has the unfortunate habit of arriving just after a decision has been made, looking around, and pointing out structural issues that would have been easier to fix earlier.

None of these three are the problem.

In fact, you would not function very well without any one of them. Remove the Inventor and you have no new ideas. Remove the Shortcutter and you would spend forty minutes deciding how to tie your shoes. Remove the Inspector and... well, you've met people who have done that.

The difficulty is not their existence.

The difficulty is their coordination.

Most of us were never taught how to run this workshop. We inherited it. We improvise. We let whichever voice is loudest at the moment take control. Sometimes that works. Sometimes it produces decisions, arguments, and beliefs that feel solid until the first good question knocks on the door.

This book is not an attempt to turn you into a perfectly rational thinker. That would require a different species.

Instead, it offers something more practical: a way to understand how your thinking is actually assembled, where it tends to bend, and how to strengthen it without losing what makes it useful in the first place.

We will look at how ideas are generated–often messily, sometimes brilliantly. We will examine the shortcuts your mind takes–why they exist, and how they quietly shape what you believe. And we will learn how to test ideas–how to distinguish between something that sounds right and something that holds up under pressure.

Along the way, you will notice a pattern.

Good thinking is not a single act.

It is a sequence.

First, ideas are created.

Then, they are filtered–sometimes helpfully, sometimes not.

Finally, they are tested.

Skip any step, and you don't have thinking.

You have a well-dressed guess.

There is, of course, a certain humility required in all of this. You will recognize your own habits in these pages. You will see thoughts you've had, arguments you've made, conclusions you've defended. Some will hold up. Others will not. That is not a failure. That is maintenance.

The goal here is not to eliminate error. That is not on offer.

The goal is to become the kind of thinker who notices it sooner.

So consider this an invitation.

Step into the workshop.

Take a look around.

Meet the crew.

And before you trust the first idea that walks in like it owns the place, let's see how it was built.

Chapter One

The Myth of the Rational Mind

If you ask most people how they make decisions, you'll hear a respectable story.

"I look at the facts."

"I weigh the options."

"I think it through."

It sounds like a panel discussion moderated by reason itself. Calm. Orderly. Sensible.

Now watch someone choose a checkout line at the grocery store.

There is a quick glance. A calculation that would embarrass a coin flip. A sudden commitment. Then, ten seconds later, a quiet suspicion that the other line is moving faster, followed by a slow lean to confirm it, as if observation might somehow reverse time.

No facts were gathered. No options were weighed. What you witnessed was something closer to instinct wearing a tie.

We do this all day.

We form impressions of people within seconds.

We decide what a headline means before finishing it.

We explain events after they happen as though we saw them coming.

And then, because we are polite creatures who like our thinking to appear respectable, we narrate the process as if it had been careful all along.

The truth is less flattering and more useful:

We are not primarily rational thinkers.

We are excellent explainers of decisions already made.

Two Speeds, One Mind

To understand this, it helps to know that your mind does not operate at one speed. It runs on two very different settings.

The first is fast. Effortless. Automatic.

It recognizes faces, finishes sentences, detects patterns, and makes snap judgments. It is always on, like a refrigerator humming in the background.

The second is slow. Deliberate. Effortful.

It solves problems, checks assumptions, and works through complexity step by careful step. It is less like a refrigerator and more like a wood stove–you have to light it, tend it, and give it time.

Thinking, Fast and Slow gave these two modes their now-famous names: System 1 and System 2.

System 1 is the fast thinker.

System 2 is the slow one.

If this sounds like a tidy division, it is not. The two systems overlap, interrupt each other, and occasionally pretend to be one another. But as a working model, it explains a great deal about why we think the way we do.

System 1 is responsible for most of what you do without noticing.

It is efficient. It is quick. It is usually good enough.

System 2, on the other hand, is what you call in when something requires real attention. It is capable of careful reasoning, but it is also lazy in the way that anything expensive tends to be. It does not volunteer unless prompted.

Left alone, System 1 will happily run the entire operation.

The Efficiency Trap

This arrangement is not a design flaw. It is a survival feature.

If you had to consciously analyze every step you took, every word you spoke, every face you recognized, you would not make it through breakfast. Fast thinking keeps you moving. It allows you to function in a world that does not wait for deliberation.

But efficiency has a cost.

Fast thinking relies on shortcuts–mental rules of thumb that simplify the world. These shortcuts are often useful. They allow you to make quick judgments with limited information.

They also allow you to be confidently wrong.

You assume a confident speaker knows what they're talking about.

You trust the first number you hear.

You remember what is vivid and forget what is merely true.

And because these judgments arrive quickly and feel natural, they do not announce themselves as guesses. They arrive as conclusions.

The Story After the Fact

Here is where things become particularly interesting.

After System 1 delivers a conclusion, System 2 often steps in–not to question it, but to explain it.

You decide you like a person.

Then you explain why they seem trustworthy.

You reject an idea.

Then you build a case against it.

You choose the checkout line.

Then you develop a theory about why it was the best option available at the time.

The explanation feels like the decision.

But it is, more often than not, a reconstruction.

We are, in this sense, natural storytellers. We do not just think–we narrate our thinking. And like all narrators, we prefer stories that are coherent, confident, and flattering to the protagonist.

The protagonist, of course, is you.

Confidence Is Not Accuracy

One of the most persistent illusions in thinking is the belief that confidence signals correctness.

It does not.

Confidence is a feeling. It is generated quickly, often by System 1, and it has very little to do with whether an idea is actually sound. A simple explanation can feel more convincing than a complex one. A familiar idea can feel more true than an unfamiliar one.

This is why people can hold strong beliefs that collapse under mild scrutiny. The belief was never tested. It was simply accepted, explained, and reinforced.

And once a belief is in place, it has a way of defending itself.

Why This Matters

At this point, you might reasonably ask: if fast thinking is flawed, why not rely on slow thinking all the time?

Because you can't.

Slow thinking is powerful, but it is also limited. It requires effort, attention, and time–resources that are in short supply. You cannot apply it to everything, and even when you try, fast thinking continues to operate in the background.

The goal, then, is not to eliminate fast thinking. That would leave you stalled at the edge of every decision.

The goal is to recognize when fast thinking is likely to lead you astray–and to know when to invite slow thinking into the room.

Back to the Workshop

If the mind is a workshop, this is where we begin to see its layout.

The fast system–the one that generates quick impressions and immediate answers–is the first to act. It is efficient, energetic, and occasionally reckless.

The slow system–the one that evaluates, checks, and reasons–is slower to arrive but essential for structural integrity.

And most of the time, the fast system hands the slow system a finished product and says, "Sign here."

If the slow system is tired, distracted, or simply not paying attention, it signs.

A Small Experiment

Try this.

The next time you have a strong opinion–about a person, an article, a decision–pause for a moment and ask:

- How quickly did this thought arrive?
- What information is it based on?
- Have I tested it, or simply accepted it?

You may find that many of your "considered" judgments were anything but.

This is not a cause for alarm. It is a starting point.

What Comes Next

In the chapters ahead, we will take this workshop apart piece by piece.

We will look at how the Inventor generates ideas–often creatively, sometimes recklessly.

We will examine how the Shortcutter shapes those ideas using mental shortcuts that can both help and mislead.

And we will learn how the Inspector can test them–when it is allowed to do its job.

For now, it is enough to set aside the myth.

You are not a perfectly rational thinker.

You are something more complicated–and far more interesting.

And if you understand how that complexity works, you can begin to use it on purpose.

Chapter Two

Meet the Crew

Every workshop has its regulars.

Not the ones listed on the payroll–the ones who are simply there. The fellow who always seems to be leaning on the bench offering suggestions. The one who cuts corners but somehow gets things done. The one in the back who inspects everything with a quiet suspicion that someone, somewhere, has made a mistake.

Your mind has these characters too.

They do not wear name tags.

They do not ask permission.

And they are involved in nearly every thought you have.

For the sake of clarity–and because it's easier to manage a crew when you can point at them–we're going to give them names:

- The Inventor
- The Shortcutter
- The Inspector

They are not separate parts of your brain in any anatomical sense. You won't find them on a scan sitting around a table. But as a working model, they explain an enormous amount about how thinking actually unfolds.

And like any crew, they do their best work when they know their role–and their worst work when they don't.

The Inventor: Patron Saint of Half-Finished Ideas

The Inventor is where ideas begin.

It is restless. Curious. Easily distracted in the most productive ways. It notices connections that are not obvious and asks questions no one else thought to ask. It is responsible for innovation, creativity,

and the occasional idea that makes you pause and say, "Now where did that come from?"

The answer, of course, is: from everywhere.

The Inventor builds ideas the way a scrap artist builds sculpture–by taking pieces from different places and assembling them into something new. A memory here, a phrase there, a half-understood concept borrowed from somewhere else, and suddenly you have a solution.

Or at least the beginnings of one.

The Inventor is not concerned with accuracy.

It is not concerned with practicality.

It is certainly not concerned with whether the idea will hold up under scrutiny.

Its job is to generate.

Give it a problem, and it will produce possibilities. Many of them. Some will be useful. Some will be nonsense. A few will be both.

Left alone, the Inventor will happily fill the workshop with prototypes–sketches, fragments, and bold declarations that have not yet met reality.

This is not a flaw.

This is the raw material of thinking.

The Shortcutter: Efficiency with a Loose Grip on Accuracy

If the Inventor is energetic, the Shortcutter is efficient.

It does not like waiting.

It does not like uncertainty.

And it has very little patience for extended analysis.

The Shortcutter's job is to get you from question to answer as quickly as possible, using the least amount of effort. It relies on patterns, habits, and familiar explanations. It fills in gaps without asking too many questions.

In many cases, this is exactly what you need.

You recognize a face without analyzing each feature.

You understand a sentence without parsing every word.

You navigate routine decisions without building a spreadsheet.

Without the Shortcutter, everyday life would grind to a halt.

But efficiency comes at a price.

The Shortcutter assumes that what worked before will work again. It leans on the first explanation that feels right. It favors what is familiar over what is accurate, what is easy over what is correct.

And because it operates quickly and quietly, it often goes unnoticed.

It does not announce, "I am making a guess."

It simply presents the guess as an answer.

The trouble is not that the Shortcutter exists.

The trouble is that it is very convincing.

The Inspector: Slow, Careful, and Frequently Ignored

Then there is the Inspector.

The Inspector is not fast. It does not offer immediate answers. It

does not generate ideas or simplify decisions. What it does is examine what has already been produced.

It asks questions.

• Does this actually make sense?

• What is the evidence?

• Are we assuming something we haven't checked?

• Does the conclusion follow from the premise, or are we skipping steps?

The Inspector is responsible for logic, structure, and careful reasoning. It is what keeps ideas from collapsing under their own weight.

It is also the least popular member of the crew.

The Inspector arrives late, speaks slowly, and has a habit of pointing out problems after everyone else has already agreed to move forward. It requires effort. It demands attention. And it often interrupts conclusions that felt perfectly satisfying a moment ago.

So it gets ignored.

Or worse, it gets recruited–not to test ideas, but to defend them.

Instead of asking, "Is this right?" the Inspector is handed a conclusion and told, "Explain why this is right."

And because it is very good at constructing arguments, it often succeeds.

When the Crew Works Well

In a well-run workshop, these three play distinct roles.

The Inventor generates ideas freely, without fear of being shut down too early.

The Shortcutter helps move things along, identifying patterns and making quick decisions where appropriate.

The Inspector steps in at the right moment to test, refine, and strengthen what has been built.

There is a rhythm to it. Ideas are generated. They are shaped. They are tested.

When this sequence holds, thinking becomes both creative and reliable. You get ideas that are not only interesting, but also sound.

When the Crew Goes Off the Rails

Most of the time, this is not what happens.

Sometimes the Inventor takes over entirely, producing a stream of ideas that are never examined. The result is creativity without structure–impressive on the surface, unstable underneath.

Sometimes the Shortcutter dominates, rushing to conclusions based on incomplete information. The result is efficiency without accuracy–quick decisions that feel right and turn out wrong.

And sometimes the Inspector is misused, brought in not to evaluate ideas but to justify them. The result is reasoning that looks rigorous but is built on untested assumptions.

In all of these cases, the problem is not the presence of any one role.

It is the absence of balance.

A Familiar Scenario

Consider a simple situation.

You meet someone new. Within moments, you have an impression.

That's the Shortcutter–quick, pattern-based, efficient.

You begin to form ideas about who they are, what they're like, how they might behave.

That's the Inventor–filling in the gaps, building a narrative.

Later, you explain your impression to someone else, offering reasons and observations that support your view.

That's the Inspector–constructing an argument.

At no point did you stop to ask whether the initial impression was accurate.

The conclusion came first.

The reasoning followed.

The First Skill: Recognition

Before you can improve how you think, you have to recognize how you're thinking.

That means noticing:

- When an idea is being generated (Inventor)
- When a shortcut is being applied (Shortcutter)
- When reasoning is being used (Inspector)

And, more importantly, noticing when one of these is doing a job it was never meant to do.

The Inventor is not a judge.

The Shortcutter is not a fact-checker.

The Inspector is not a spokesperson.

Back to Work

By now, you may have recognized these characters in your own thinking.

You've had ideas that felt brilliant the moment they appeared.

You've made decisions that seemed obvious at the time.

You've constructed arguments that sounded convincing–until someone asked a better question.

That's not a flaw in your thinking. That is your thinking.

The goal is not to replace this crew. It's to manage it.

In the next chapters, we'll spend time with each of them–first the

Inventor, then the Shortcutter, then the Inspector–understanding not just what they do, but how they do it, and how to use them without letting them run the place.

For now, it's enough to know this:

You are not a single voice in your own head.

You are the foreman of a busy, opinionated workshop.

And the sooner you learn who's holding which tool, the fewer surprises you'll find when the work is done.

Chapter Three

Why Your Brain Loves Shortcuts

There is a noble idea floating around that the mind seeks truth.

It does not. It seeks efficiency.

Truth is welcome when it arrives quickly and without fuss. But if truth requires effort, patience, and the uncomfortable admission that you might be wrong, the mind begins to look around for a more convenient option.

And usually, it finds one.

The Cost of Thinking

Thinking–real thinking–is expensive.

It requires attention, and attention is a limited resource. It requires time, and time has a way of running short just when you need it. It requires effort, and effort is something the brain tries to conserve like a careful household budget.

So the mind develops shortcuts.

Not out of laziness, exactly. Out of necessity.

Imagine if every decision required full analysis:

- Which route should I take to work?
- What does this sentence mean?
- Is this person trustworthy?

If each question demanded a careful, step-by-step evaluation, you would spend the better part of your day stalled in place, staring thoughtfully at doorknobs.

Shortcuts keep things moving.

They allow you to function in a world that does not pause while you deliberate.

Heuristics: The Brain's Rulebook

These shortcuts have a proper name: heuristics.

That word makes them sound respectable, which is appropriate, because they are. Heuristics are simple rules your brain uses to make decisions quickly.

- If it's familiar, it's probably safe.
- If it comes to mind easily, it must be common.
- If it sounds confident, it's probably correct.

None of these are guaranteed to be true.

But they are often useful enough.

And that, as it turns out, is the standard your brain is aiming for.

Not perfect.

Not even particularly accurate.

Just good enough to get you through the moment.

The Efficiency Trade-Off

Every shortcut is a trade. You gain speed. You lose precision.

Most of the time, this trade works in your favor. You make quick, reasonably accurate decisions without expending much effort. You recognize patterns, navigate familiar situations, and respond to routine problems with minimal strain.

But when the situation is unfamiliar, complex, or misleading, those same shortcuts can lead you astray.

You remember the dramatic event and assume it is common.

You accept the first number you hear and build your thinking around it. You trust your initial impression and never revisit it.

And because the shortcut delivered an answer quickly, it feels right.

That feeling is persuasive. It is also unreliable.

The Comfort of Easy Thinking

There is a physical sensation to thinking.

Effortful thinking feels… effortful. It slows you down. It requires concentration. It introduces doubt.

Easy thinking feels smooth. It flows. It gives you the quiet satisfaction of understanding without the inconvenience of work.

The brain prefers the second.

This preference is so strong that it will often choose an easy answer over a correct one, simply because it fits more comfortably.

You see this in small ways:

A statement that is easy to read feels more true than one that is complex. A familiar idea feels more accurate than a new one.

A repeated claim begins to sound like a fact. Ease is mistaken for evidence.

When the Shortcutter Takes Over

This is the domain of the Shortcutter–the part of your thinking that relies on heuristics to move quickly from question to answer.

It is not malicious. It is not careless. It is doing exactly what it was designed to do: conserve effort and produce results.

But it has two habits that cause trouble.

First, it does not announce when it is using a shortcut.

You are not told, "This is a quick guess based on limited information."

You are told, "This is the answer."

Second, it does not revisit its conclusions unless prompted.

Once a shortcut has produced a result, the mind tends to accept it and move on. There is no automatic second check. No built-in pause for reflection.

Unless, of course, something forces one.

Predictable Irrationality

Here's the interesting part: these shortcuts do not lead to random errors. They lead to predictable ones.

People tend to make the same kinds of mistakes, in the same situations, for the same reasons. This is why patterns of irrational behavior can be studied, measured, and, to some extent, anticipated.

As explored in *Predictably Irrational*, our decisions are not simply flawed–they are flawed in consistent ways.

We overvalue what we already own. We are influenced by irrelevant numbers. We make different choices depending on how options are framed.

These are not isolated lapses. They are features of the system.

The Illusion of Knowing

One of the more subtle consequences of shortcuts is the illusion that you understand something more fully than you do.

You read a brief explanation. You grasp the general idea. You feel as though you know it. But when asked to explain it in detail, the gaps appear.

The shortcut gave you a sense of understanding without the substance. This is not deception in the usual sense. It is compression.

The brain reduces complexity to something manageable and then mistakes the simplified version for the whole.

A Quiet Example

Consider this question:

Why do airplanes fly?

Most people have a general sense of the answer. Something about wings, air pressure, lift. It feels familiar. Comfortable.

Now try to explain it clearly, step by step, without skipping anything. You may find that what felt like understanding was, in fact, a collection of fragments held together by confidence.

That's the Shortcutter at work.

When to Be Suspicious

Shortcuts are not the enemy. They are essential. But there are moments when you should become suspicious of your own thinking:

- When an answer comes immediately and feels obvious
- When a conclusion aligns perfectly with what you already believe
- When a complex issue seems suddenly simple
- When confidence arrives before evidence

These are signals–not that you are wrong, but that you may not have looked closely enough.

Inviting the Inspector

This is where the Inspector becomes important.

The Shortcutter will not slow down on its own. It needs to be interrupted. It needs a reason to pause, to reconsider, to examine what it has produced.

That reason is usually a question.

- How do I know this?
- What information am I missing?
- Could there be another explanation?

These questions are not dramatic. They do not require a complete overhaul of your thinking. They simply create a moment of friction–a small resistance that prevents you from moving forward too quickly.

And in that moment, better thinking becomes possible.

Back to the Workshop

In the workshop, the Shortcutter is the one who says, "That'll do," before the glue has fully set.

Most of the time, it's right. The chair holds. The door closes. The job gets done.But occasionally, the leg wobbles. The hinge sticks. The structure reveals its weakness under pressure.

Not because the work was rushed maliciously–but because it was rushed at all.

What Comes Next

Understanding shortcuts is only the beginning.

In the next section, we'll take a closer look at the patterns these shortcuts create–the biases that shape how we see the world, often without our awareness.

If shortcuts are the tools, biases are the habits.

And habits, once formed, have a way of repeating themselves.

For now, it's enough to remember this:

Your brain is not trying to mislead you.

It is trying to help you move quickly.

But speed is not the same as accuracy.

And when the answer arrives too easily, it may be worth asking how it was built before you decide to trust

Chapter Four

Where Ideas Come From

If you ask someone where their ideas come from, you will usually get one of two answers.

The first is poetic.

"They just come to me."

The second is evasive.

"I don't know, they just do."

Both are unsatisfying, but not entirely wrong.

Ideas often feel like they arrive out of nowhere–fully formed, unannounced, as if your mind had been quietly working a night shift without informing you. One moment there is nothing. The next, there it is: a solution, a phrase, a connection that seems obvious now that it exists.

The trouble is, this feeling of suddenness hides the actual process.

Ideas do not come from nowhere.

They come from everywhere you've ever been paying attention.

The Scrap Heap of the Mind

The Inventor–the part of your thinking responsible for generating ideas–does not build from scratch. It builds from pieces.

Memories. Observations. Half-understood concepts.

Things you read last week and forgot you read. Things you noticed ten years ago and assumed were gone. Nothing is wasted.

The mind keeps a sprawling, disorganized inventory of fragments. And when a problem presents itself, the Inventor begins rummaging.

It pulls a piece from one place, another from somewhere else, and tries to fit them together. Sometimes the pieces align cleanly.

Sometimes they require a bit of forcing. Occasionally, they don't fit at all–but the Inventor will try anyway. This is why ideas often feel familiar.Because they are.

They are new arrangements of old material.

Association: The Quiet Engine

At the center of this process is association. One thought leads to another, not by logic, but by proximity, similarity, or sheer coincidence. You think of a word, which reminds you of a phrase, which brings to mind a story, which suggests a solution.

The path is rarely straight.It zigzags. And that zigzagging is not a flaw–it is the mechanism itself.

Creative thinking depends on the ability to move between ideas that are not obviously connected. To see a relationship where none is immediately apparent. To treat distant concepts as if they might belong in the same sentence.

This is what makes the Inventor both valuable and, at times, unpredictable.

Lateral Thinking: Leaving the Obvious Behind

Most of our thinking follows established paths. We approach problems the way we've approached similar problems before. We apply known solutions. We stay within familiar boundaries.

This works–until it doesn't.

When a problem resists the usual approach, the Inventor has to do something different. It has to step sideways.

This is the essence of what Lateral Thinking calls lateral thinking–a deliberate attempt to move away from obvious patterns and explore alternative routes.

Instead of asking, "What is the correct answer?"

You ask, "What are other ways to look at this?"

Instead of following the straight line, you take a detour.

Not because the detour is efficient, but because it might reveal something the straight line cannot.

The Role of Constraints

There is a common belief that creativity thrives on freedom. Give people complete freedom, the thinking goes, and they will produce their best work.

Experience suggests otherwise.

Too much freedom can be paralyzing. With no boundaries, the Inventor has nothing to push against. The possibilities become so wide that they lose definition.

Constraints, on the other hand, give shape to thinking.

- Write a story in exactly 500 words
- Solve the problem without using the usual method
- Explain the idea to someone with no background knowledge

These limits force the Inventor to work differently. To recombine ideas in ways it might not otherwise consider. A constraint is not a restriction. It is a direction.

Bad Ideas as Raw Material

One of the quieter truths about creativity is that good ideas are often built on bad ones.

The Inventor produces freely. It does not sort or filter in real time. That means many of its outputs are incomplete, impractical, or simply wrong. This is not a problem unless you expect every idea to be good.

If you treat each idea as a finished product, you will become cautious. You will generate fewer ideas, and the ones you do produce will stay close to what is already known.

If, instead, you treat ideas as raw material, the process changes.

A bad idea is not a failure. It is a starting point. It can be refined, combined, or discarded–but it contributes to the process. The workshop fills with prototypes, and from those prototypes, something useful eventually emerges.

The Timing Problem

The Inventor works best under certain conditions.It does not respond well to pressure that demands immediate correctness.

It does not thrive under constant evaluation. And it tends to shut down when every idea is judged the moment it appears.

This creates a timing problem.

If the Inspector–the part of your thinking that evaluates ideas–arrives too early, it can stop the process before it has a chance to develop. Ideas are dismissed before they have time to take shape.

On the other hand, if the Inspector never arrives, the workshop fills with unfinished, untested ideas that may sound impressive but lack substance.

Good thinking requires sequence. First, generation.Then, evaluation.

Not both at once.

A Familiar Experience

You've likely had this happen. You're working on a problem, making little progress. The ideas feel forced. Nothing quite fits. Then you step away.

You go for a walk. You do something unrelated. You stop trying. And suddenly, the solution appears.

It feels like magic.But it isn't.

While you were occupied elsewhere, the Inventor was still at work–quietly sorting, connecting, and recombining ideas without the interference of immediate judgment. When the pieces finally aligned, the result surfaced.

The delay was not inactivity. It was incubation.

The Risk of Loving Your Ideas Too Much

There is, however, a danger in this process.

Ideas that arrive suddenly, especially after effort or frustration, tend to feel valuable. They carry a sense of ownership. You discovered them. You assembled them. They feel like yours. And because they feel like yours, they are harder to question.

The Inventor, left unchecked, becomes attached to its creations. It begins to defend them, to favor them, to assume they are better than they might actually be.

This is where the next stage becomes critical. Because no matter how an idea arrives–quickly or slowly, effortlessly or through effort–it still needs to be tested.

Back to the Workshop

In the workshop, the Inventor is the one spreading materials across the table, sketching possibilities, trying combinations that may or may not work.

It is energetic. Generous. Slightly chaotic. It produces far more than will ever be used. And that is exactly what it should do.

The mistake is not in having too many ideas. The mistake is in assuming that the first good one is the right one.

What Comes Next

Now that we've seen how ideas are generated, we turn to what happens next. Because ideas do not move directly from creation to truth.

They pass through another layer first–the Shortcutter–where patterns are applied, assumptions are made, and biases begin to shape what survives.

If the Inventor fills the workshop with possibilities, the Shortcutter begins deciding which ones feel right. And as we'll see, what feels right is not always what is right.

For now, remember this:

Ideas are not discovered fully formed. They are assembled. And the quality of what you build depends not just on what you create, but on what you do with it next.

Chapter Five

Breaking the Obvious

Most thinking follows a well-worn path. You see a problem. You reach for a familiar approach. You apply what has worked before and hope it works again. And most of the time, it does.

Which is precisely the problem.

Because the obvious path is not just well-worn–it's crowded. Everyone else has been there already. The solutions along that route are known, predictable, and, more often than not, already in use.

If you want a different result, you have to leave the path. Not dramatically. Not recklessly. Just… deliberately.

The Gravity of the First Idea

When faced with a problem, the first idea that comes to mind has a certain authority. It arrives quickly. It feels natural. It often resembles something that has worked before. And because of all this, it tends to stick.

This is the gravity of the first idea. It pulls your thinking into orbit around it. Everything that follows is shaped in relation to that initial answer–refining it, adjusting it, defending it.

Very rarely do we discard it entirely. This is efficient. It is also limiting. Because the first idea is usually the most obvious one. And the obvious solution is, by definition, the one most accessible to everyone.

Why Obvious Thinking Feels Right

Obvious ideas feel right because they are easy to access. They are built from familiar patterns. They require little effort to assemble. They fit neatly into what you already know. There is a sense of fluency to them–a smoothness that the mind interprets as correctness.

But fluency is not accuracy. It is simply ease. And ease has a way of disguising itself as insight.

Stepping Sideways

To move beyond the obvious, you don't need a flash of genius. You need a willingness to step sideways.

This is the core of lateral thinking–not abandoning logic, but postponing it long enough to explore alternatives that would normally be dismissed.

Lateral Thinking introduced this idea as a deliberate process. Not inspiration, not luck, but a method.

Instead of asking:

- What is the right answer?

You ask:

- What are other ways to look at this?
- What assumptions am I making?
- What if the opposite were true?

These questions don't guarantee a better answer. They simply open more doors.

Challenging Assumptions

Every problem arrives with a set of assumptions attached.

Some are obvious. Some are invisible.All of them shape how you approach the solution.

For example:

- This is how it's always been done
- These are the constraints we have
- This is what the problem actually is

The difficulty is that assumptions rarely introduce themselves.

They sit quietly in the background, influencing your thinking without announcing their presence.

Breaking the obvious often begins with identifying these hidden boundaries.

- What if the constraint isn't real?
- What if the problem has been defined incorrectly?
- What if the goal itself is wrong?

These questions can feel disruptive. They unsettle what seemed stable. That's the point.

Techniques for Leaving the Path

There are simple ways to nudge the Inventor out of its usual patterns. None of them are complicated. Most of them feel slightly unnatural at first–which is a good sign.

1. Reverse the Problem

Instead of asking how to solve it, ask how to make it worse.

Then examine those answers. Often, they reveal assumptions and overlooked factors.

2. Change the Frame

Describe the problem in a completely different way. A business problem becomes a storytelling problem. A logistical issue becomes a design challenge. New frames suggest new solutions.

3. Force a Connection

Take two unrelated ideas and ask how they might connect. Most combinations won't work. That's fine. The goal is not immediate success–it's movement.

4. Add a Constraint

Limit time, resources, or methods. Constraints force the Inventor to work differently, often producing ideas that wouldn't emerge under normal conditions.

The Discomfort of New Thinking

There is a moment, when you move away from the obvious, where thinking becomes uncomfortable. The path is less clear. The ideas are less certain. The confidence that accompanied the first solution fades.

This is often mistaken for failure. It isn't. It's the absence of familiarity.

The mind prefers what it recognizes. When you step outside that, you lose the reassuring sense that you're on the right track. But this discomfort is a signal that you've left the well-worn path. And that's where new ideas live.

A Quiet Example

Consider something simple: improving a classroom. The obvious solutions might be:

- Better materials
- More time
- Smaller class sizes

All reasonable. All familiar. Now step sideways.

- What if the students taught part of the lesson?
- What if the classroom wasn't a classroom?
- What if silence was used differently?

Not all of these ideas will work. Some will fail outright. But in exploring them, you begin to see the problem differently. And in seeing it differently, you increase the chances of finding something that does work.

The Risk of Wandering Too Far

Of course, there is a limit. If you move too far from the original problem, you risk losing it entirely. Ideas become disconnected, impractical, or irrelevant.

This is where the next stage–the Inspector–becomes essential.

Creative thinking expands possibilities. Logical thinking refines them.

Without expansion, you get predictable answers. Without refinement, you get unusable ones.

Back to the Workshop

In the workshop, breaking the obvious is the moment when the Inventor stops building the same chair it has built a hundred times and starts experimenting.

- Maybe the legs are arranged differently.
- Maybe the material changes.
- Maybe it's not a chair at all.

Most of these experiments won't make it to the showroom. But one of them might. And that one would not have appeared if the Inventor had stayed on the familiar path.

What Comes Next

Now that we've seen how to generate ideas and move beyond the obvious, we turn to the force that quietly shapes which ideas survive. Because not all ideas are treated equally.

Some feel right immediately. Others are dismissed just as quickly. This is not because they are better or worse. It is because the Shortcutter has preferences.

In the next chapter, we'll begin to examine those preferences–the biases that influence what you accept, what you reject, and what you never question at all.

For now, remember this:

The first idea is rarely the best one. It is simply the easiest one to reach. And if you want better thinking, you have to be willing to take a few steps beyond it–even if the ground feels unfamiliar at first.

Chapter Six

The Problem with Cleverness

There is a particular kind of idea that arrives with a flourish.

It is elegant. It is surprising. It has just enough novelty to feel original and just enough familiarity to feel right. It is, in a word, clever. And clever ideas are dangerous.

Not because they are wrong.Many of them aren't. But because they feel more correct than they have any right to.

The Seduction of a Good Idea

When the Inventor produces something clever, it tends to land with confidence. You see the connection. You appreciate the twist. You feel the satisfaction of having arrived somewhere interesting. And that feeling does something subtle.

It lowers your guard.

The idea doesn't just seem promising, it seems finished. As though the work of thinking has already been done.

But cleverness is not completion. It's presentation.

Why Clever Ideas Stick

Clever ideas have three advantages that make them particularly persuasive:

1. They are memorable

They stand out from ordinary thinking. They have a shape, a twist, a quality that makes them easy to recall.

2. They are satisfying

They resolve tension. They offer a neat explanation. They give the impression of insight.

3. They signal intelligence

Both to you and to others. A clever idea feels like evidence that you, or the person presenting it, are thinking at a higher level.

All of this creates a powerful effect:

The idea is accepted quickly, repeated confidently, and rarely examined closely.

The Difference Between Clever and Correct

A clever idea often compresses complexity into something simple. That's part of its appeal.

But in that compression, details are lost. Assumptions are hidden. Gaps are smoothed over. The result is an explanation that feels complete, even when it isn't.

Consider how often you hear a statement like:

- "People do this because…"
- "The reason is simple…"
- "It all comes down to…"

These phrases signal closure. They promise clarity. And sometimes they deliver it.

But just as often, they reduce a complex situation to a single cause that happens to sound good.

Cleverness favors simplicity. Reality rarely cooperates.

The Overconfidence Problem

There is a quiet escalation that happens once a clever idea takes hold.

First, it is interesting. Then, it is convincing. Finally, it becomes obvious.At that point, questioning it feels unnecessary. Even unreasonable. After all, the idea makes sense. It fits. It explains things.

What more is there to do?

Quite a bit, as it turns out.

Because the confidence attached to the idea has grown faster than the evidence supporting it.

When Creativity Turns Inward

There is another risk.

The same Inventor that generated the idea is very good at defending it. Once you become attached to a clever idea, your thinking begins to shift. Instead of asking, "Is this right?" you begin asking, "How can I show this is right?"

You generate supporting examples. You notice confirming evidence. You explain away contradictions.

In other words, creativity turns inward. It stops producing alternatives and starts reinforcing the current idea. This is where the Shortcutter and the Inventor quietly form an alliance.

One provides the quick acceptance. The other provides the convincing explanation. And together, they can build a very sturdy illusion.

A Familiar Pattern

You've likely seen this play out.

Someone presents an idea that reframes a situation in a new way. It's insightful. It connects dots that weren't previously connected.

Everyone nods.

The idea spreads.

Soon, it becomes the explanation.

And only later–if at all–does someone ask whether the connections were justified, whether the explanation holds up, whether alternative explanations were considered.

By that point, the idea has momentum.

And momentum is difficult to interrupt.

The Role of the Inspector

This is where the Inspector must be invited in–not as an afterthought, but as a necessary step.

The Inspector does not care how clever an idea is. It does not care how satisfying it feels. It asks only one question:

Does it hold up?

- Are the assumptions valid?
- Is the evidence sufficient?
- Does the conclusion follow logically?

These questions are not dramatic. They do not diminish the creativity of the idea. They simply test its structure.

A clever idea that survives inspection becomes something more valuable: a sound idea.

A clever idea that does not survive inspection becomes something else: a useful lesson.

Separating Identity from Ideas

One of the reasons clever ideas are difficult to test is that they feel personal. You came up with it. You shaped it. You recognize its elegance. Questioning the idea can feel like questioning your ability to think.

This is a mistake.

An idea is not a reflection of your worth. It is a product of your thinking. And like any product, it can be improved, revised, or discarded. The more closely you tie your identity to your ideas, the harder it becomes to examine them honestly.

The workshop becomes less a place of construction and more a place of defense.

A Simple Practice

When you encounter a clever idea–your own or someone else's–pause and ask:

- What assumptions does this rely on?
- What would have to be true for this to work?
- What might this be missing?

These questions do not reject the idea. They slow it down. And slowing down is often enough to reveal whether the idea is as solid as it first appeared.

Back to the Workshop

In the workshop, cleverness is the moment when something comes together beautifully. The lines are clean. The joints fit. The design is appealing. Everyone steps back and admires it.

That's fine. But admiration is not inspection.

Before the piece leaves the shop, it still needs to be tested. Sat on. Pressed. Used. Because a chair that looks perfect but collapses under weight is not a success.

It's a demonstration.

What Comes Next

We've now seen how ideas are generated and how they can become convincing before they are confirmed.

Next, we turn to the force that quietly shapes these ideas from the moment they appear–the patterns and biases that influence what we notice, what we believe, and what we ignore.

If cleverness is the surface, bias is the current underneath. And it is far more powerful than it appears.

For now, remember this:

A clever idea earns your attention. It does not earn your trust.

That still has to be built.

Chapter Seven

The Brain as a Pattern Machine

Give the human mind a handful of scattered dots, and it will draw a line.

Give it a few lines, and it will invent a shape.

Give it a shape, and it will tell you what it means.

This is not a flaw. It is the operating system.

The Hunger for Pattern

Long before we built cities or wrote books or argued about ideas, we were creatures trying to make sense of a noisy world.

- The rustle in the grass–wind or predator?
- The change in the sky–weather or warning?
- The unfamiliar face–friend or threat?

Waiting for complete information was not an option. Survival favored those who could recognize patterns quickly, even if those patterns were occasionally wrong.

Better to see a pattern that isn't there than to miss one that is. That instinct never left.

It followed us into modern life, where the dangers are different but the machinery is the same. The brain still scans, connects, predicts. It still tries to turn fragments into meaning as efficiently as possible.

Seeing What Isn't There

This is why we see faces in clouds, figures in shadows, meaning in coincidence. A stock market rises for three days in a row, and we begin to detect a trend. Two events occur close together, and we assume one caused the other.

A person behaves in a certain way once, and we begin to build a story about who they are.

The mind is not content with randomness. It prefers a pattern, even an invented one, over uncertainty.

Pattern Recognition vs Pattern Invention

There is a difference, though, between recognizing a real pattern and inventing one.

Pattern recognition is valuable. It allows you to learn, to anticipate, to understand how things tend to behave.

Pattern invention is something else. It takes limited or ambiguous information and imposes structure where none may exist.

The difficulty is that both feel the same.

When a pattern appears in your thinking, it arrives with a sense of clarity. It feels like insight. It gives the impression that something has been understood. But that feeling does not tell you whether the pattern is real. It only tells you that the mind has found a way to connect the pieces.

The Speed of Meaning

Pattern-making happens quickly. You do not consciously assemble each step. You do not weigh alternative explanations. The connection simply appears. And because it appears so easily, it feels trustworthy.

This is the Shortcutter at work–using past experience, familiarity, and mental shortcuts to generate meaning without requiring effortful analysis.

It is efficient. It is also prone to error.

The Comfort of Coherence

A pattern brings with it a sense of coherence. Things fit together. Events make sense. The world feels less random, less chaotic.

This is deeply satisfying. We prefer a coherent story, even if it is incomplete or slightly inaccurate, to a collection of disconnected facts.

A narrative fills the gaps. A pattern explains the noise. And once that coherence is established, it becomes difficult to unsettle.

When Patterns Mislead

The problem arises when patterns are assumed rather than tested.

You notice that successful people share certain traits and conclude that those traits cause success. You observe a sequence of events and assume they are linked. You generalize from a small number of examples to a broader rule.

In each case, the mind has done what it does best: it has connected the dots. But it has not asked whether the dots belong together.

A Quiet Example

Imagine flipping a coin five times and getting heads each time.

A pattern appears. It feels as though something is happening–that the coin is "on a streak," that tails is "due," or that something unusual is at work.

In reality, each flip is independent. But the mind resists that explanation. It prefers a pattern to pure chance.

Randomness feels unsatisfying. A pattern feels meaningful. So the mind supplies one.

The Role of Experience

Patterns are not always wrong. In fact, they are often based on real experience.

You learn that certain behaviors lead to certain outcomes. You recognize familiar situations. You develop an intuitive sense of how things tend to unfold.

This is expertise. But expertise can also create blind spots.

When you expect a pattern, you are more likely to see it–even when it isn't there. You interpret new information through the lens of past experience, sometimes forcing it to fit.

The pattern becomes not just a tool, but a filter.

The Illusion of Understanding

When a pattern takes hold, it creates the feeling that you understand something. The situation seems clear. The explanation seems sufficient. The uncertainty fades.

But this understanding can be shallow. It may rest on limited evidence. It may ignore alternative explanations. It may simplify complexity into something manageable but incomplete.

The pattern gives you a story. Whether that story is accurate is another matter.

Interrupting the Pattern

The challenge is not to stop seeing patterns. That would be impossible. The challenge is to question them.

When a pattern appears, especially one that feels obvious, it is worth asking:

- What evidence supports this pattern?
- What evidence might contradict it?
- Could this be coincidence rather than cause?
- Are there other ways to interpret this?

These questions do not eliminate patterns. They test them. And in that testing, the Inspector begins to do its work.

Back to the Workshop

In the workshop, the pattern machine is the part that looks at a pile of materials and says, "I've seen something like this before."

Sometimes that's exactly right. The pieces fit. The structure holds.

Other times, the resemblance is superficial. The materials behave differently. The design doesn't quite translate.

But the pattern feels familiar, so the work proceeds as if it were the same.

Until it isn't.

What Comes Next

Now that we've seen how the mind creates patterns, we can begin to examine the specific ways those patterns shape our thinking. Because patterns, once established, become habits. And those habits: confirmation bias, availability, anchoring, and others, quietly influence what we notice, what we believe, and what we ignore.

If the brain is a pattern machine, bias is the set of patterns it prefers.And understanding those preferences is the next step in understanding how we think.

For now, remember this:

A pattern is a possibility. It is not a conclusion.

And the moment it feels obvious is often the moment it deserves a closer look.

Chapter Eight

A Field Guide to Fooling Yourself

By now, you've met the Shortcutter. Efficient. Confident. A little too quick to say, "That makes sense."

In this chapter, we'll take a closer look at its favorite tools–the recurring patterns of error that show up so reliably you could almost set your watch by them.

These are called cognitive biases. That phrase sounds technical, but the idea is simple:

A bias is a predictable way your thinking bends. Not randomly. Not occasionally. Predictably.And once you know the bends, you start to see them everywhere, like noticing the slight lean in a row of old houses that have settled just enough to tell a story.

Why a Field Guide?

Because biases don't arrive with labels. They don't announce themselves as mistakes. They feel like normal thinking.

A field guide doesn't eliminate them. It helps you recognize them when they appear: mid-thought, mid-decision, mid-conversation.

Not after the fact. During. So consider this a walk through familiar territory, pointing out what has been there all along.

1. Confirmation Bias: Seeing What You Came to See

This is the classic.

You form an opinion. Then you look for evidence that supports it. You notice the articles that agree with you. You remember the examples that reinforce your view. You dismiss or overlook anything that doesn't fit.

It feels like research. It is, more often, selection.

Confirmation bias doesn't create your beliefs. It protects them.

It turns the mind into a curator, carefully arranging evidence that tells a consistent story while quietly removing anything that complicates it. And because the resulting picture is coherent, it feels convincing.

2. Availability Heuristic: What Comes Easily Must Be Common

Ask yourself: how dangerous is flying compared to driving? Most people will hesitate. Not because they don't know the statistics, but because what comes to mind matters more than what is true.

Plane crashes are vivid. They are reported, repeated, remembered.

Car accidents are ordinary. They happen constantly, and precisely because of that, they fade into the background.

The mind uses availability–how easily something comes to mind–as a shortcut for frequency and importance. If you can recall it quickly, it must matter. If you can't, it must not.

This is efficient. It is also misleading.

3. Anchoring: The First Number Sticks

The first piece of information you encounter has a peculiar influence. It sets a reference point–an anchor–from which everything else is judged.

Consider a simple scenario:

You see a product listed at $500, marked down to $300.

The second number feels like a bargain. Not because $300 is inherently reasonable, but because it is compared to the first number.Remove the anchor, and the perception changes.

Anchoring works the same way in negotiations, estimates, and everyday decisions. The initial figure, however arbitrary, shapes what follows. And once it's in place, it is remarkably difficult to ignore.

4. Framing: The Same Facts, Different Story

How something is presented matters as much as what is presented.

A treatment with a 90% survival rate sounds reassuring.

The same treatment with a 10% mortality rate feels risky.

The numbers are identical. The interpretation is not.

Framing changes the emotional tone of information. It highlights certain aspects while downplaying others. And because we respond not just to facts but to how those facts are described, framing quietly guides decisions without altering the underlying reality.

5. The Narrative Bias: Turning Events into Stories

The mind prefers stories to fragments.

A sequence of events becomes a cause-and-effect chain. A coincidence becomes a meaningful connection. A complex situation becomes a simple explanation.

Stories provide coherence. They make the world feel understandable.

But in doing so, they often smooth over uncertainty, ignore randomness, and impose structure where none exists.

We don't just experience events. We arrange them. And once arranged, they feel inevitable.

The Pattern Beneath the Patterns

Each of these biases looks different on the surface, but they share a common function:

- They simplify.
- They reduce complexity.
- They speed up decisions.
- They make the world easier to navigate.

And most of the time, that's useful.

But simplification comes at a cost. Details are lost. Alternatives are ignored. Uncertainty is replaced with confidence.

The Shortcutter does not ask, "Is this the most accurate way to think about this?"

It asks, "Is this good enough to move forward?"

Why These Biases Persist

If these patterns lead to errors, why do they persist?

Because they work–just not perfectly.

They allow you to make quick decisions in a complex world. They reduce the burden on slow, effortful thinking. They provide a sense of understanding even when information is incomplete.

In short, they are efficient. And efficiency is what the mind values most of the time.

Recognizing the Bend

The goal is not to eliminate bias. That would require more effort than the brain is willing to provide.

The goal is to recognize when your thinking may be bending.

That recognition often begins with small signals:

- When you only notice information that supports your view
- When vivid examples outweigh quiet data
- When the first number feels strangely important
- When a story feels too neat, too complete

These are not proof of error. They are invitations to look again.

A Practical Pause

When you encounter a decision or a belief that feels obvious, try a simple pause:

- What might I be overlooking?
- What would I think if the initial information were different?
- Am I reacting to how this is presented, or to what is actually true?

These questions do not dismantle bias entirely.

But they slow it down.

And slowing it down is often enough to let better thinking in.

Back to the Workshop

In the workshop, biases are the habits that develop over time.

The way a cut is made without measuring. The way a tool is used because it's always been used that way. The way a problem is approached because it looks familiar.

Most of the time, these habits produce acceptable results.

But occasionally, they produce the same mistake–over and over again–because no one stopped to question the method.

What Comes Next

We've seen how biases shape what we notice and what we believe.

Next, we'll look at how those biases extend into something more structured–how they influence not just our perceptions, but the arguments we make and accept.Because when bias enters reasoning, it doesn't just bend thoughts.

It builds them. And what it builds can look remarkably solid–until you examine the foundation.

For now, remember this:

You are not just thinking. You are thinking in patterns.

And some of those patterns, left unchecked, will quietly lead you exactly where you expected to go.

Chapter Nine

The Stories We Can't Stop Telling

If patterns are the mind's raw material, stories are what it builds with them.

We do not live among isolated facts. We arrange them.

We take events, impressions, fragments of information–and we stitch them together into something that feels whole. Something that has a beginning, a middle, and, if we're lucky, an ending that makes sense.

This is not a hobby. It is how we understand the world.

From Events to Explanations

Something happens. You miss a deadline. A conversation goes poorly. A decision works out–or doesn't. Almost immediately, the mind begins to explain it.

- I was rushed.
- They were difficult.
- It worked because I planned well.

These explanations arrive quickly, often without effort. They connect the dots. They turn an event into a story. And once the story is in place, it feels complete.

But the speed of the explanation should give you pause because the story didn't emerge from careful analysis.

It emerged from the same machinery that builds patterns and applies shortcuts.

The Narrative Bias

We are inclined to believe that events follow clear causes. This leads to what's often called the narrative bias–the tendency to create coherent stories from incomplete information.

We prefer:

- Simple causes over complex ones
- Clear sequences over randomness
- Intentions over accidents

A messy reality is reorganized into something tidy. And tidy is persuasive.

The Trouble with Coherence

A good story has a certain shape.

It flows. It connects. It resolves.

The problem is that real life rarely behaves that way.

Events are influenced by multiple factors. Outcomes are shaped by chance as much as by intention. Sequences are often incomplete or misleading. But the mind resists that uncertainty.

It fills in gaps. It smooths over contradictions. It removes the rough edges that don't fit the narrative. What remains is a story that makes sense–even if it isn't entirely accurate.

After the Fact

One of the most reliable features of storytelling is that it happens after the fact. An outcome occurs. Then we explain it.

This creates a subtle illusion:

It feels as though the explanation was always there, as though the outcome was predictable, even inevitable. But that sense of inevitability is constructed in hindsight.

Before the event, there were multiple possibilities. After the event, there is only one story.

And that story, once formed, tends to overwrite the uncertainty that preceded it.

The Illusion of Cause

Stories are built on cause and effect. This happened because of that.

But identifying cause is more difficult than it appears. Just because two events are connected in a story does not mean one caused the other.

- A business succeeds after a new strategy is implemented
- A student improves after a change in routine
- A market shifts after a particular announcement

In each case, it is tempting to assign a clear cause. But reality is rarely so cooperative. Multiple factors are at play. Some visible, some not. Some significant, some incidental.

The story selects one.

Identity and Story

The most persistent stories are the ones we tell about ourselves.

Who we are. What we're good at. Why we succeed or fail.

These stories are built from experience, but they are shaped by interpretation. A success becomes evidence of ability. A failure becomes evidence of circumstance–or the other way around, depending on the story.

Over time, these narratives solidify. They guide decisions. They influence behavior. They shape what we attempt and what we avoid.

And because they feel personal, they are rarely questioned.

The Comfort of Explanation

A story does something important. It removes uncertainty.

When something happens and you don't understand why, there is a gap. That gap is uncomfortable. It leaves room for doubt, for multiple possibilities, for the unsettling idea that things might not be as clear as they seem.

A story closes that gap. It replaces uncertainty with explanation.

Even if the explanation is incomplete, it is often preferred to having no explanation at all.

A Quiet Example

Imagine a team wins a game. Afterward, the story emerges:

They won because of strong leadership. Because of preparation. Because of discipline. All of these may be true.

But they are not the whole picture.

There were missed opportunities, random events, small moments that could have gone differently. If they had, the story would change.

The outcome shapes the explanation. Not the other way around.

When Stories Become Traps

Stories are useful.

They help us organize information, communicate ideas, and make sense of experience. But they can also become traps. Once a story is established, it becomes the lens through which new information is interpreted.

Evidence that fits the story is accepted. Evidence that doesn't is questioned or ignored. The story becomes self-reinforcing. And over time, it can become difficult to see beyond it.

Interrupting the Narrative

The goal is not to stop telling stories. That would leave us with disconnected fragments and no way to understand them.

The goal is to recognize when a story may be doing more than organizing information–when it may be simplifying, distorting, or closing off alternative explanations.

When you find yourself explaining an event, it can help to ask:

- What else might explain this?
- What details have I left out?
- Am I assuming cause where there may only be correlation?
- How would this story change if the outcome were different?

These questions do not dismantle the story. They loosen it. They allow space for complexity.

Back to the Workshop

In the workshop, stories are the finished pieces–the assembled structures that give meaning to the materials. They look complete. They feel solid.

But if you examine them closely, you may find joints that were filled rather than fitted, connections that were assumed rather than secured. The structure holds–for now. But without inspection, you don't know how much weight it can bear.

What Comes Next

We've seen how patterns lead to biases, and how biases shape the stories we tell. Now we turn to what happens when those stories become arguments–when we present them, defend them, and rely on them to persuade. Because once a story is expressed as reasoning, it takes on a new form.

It becomes something that can be tested. Or something that should be. For now, remember this:

A story explains what happened. It does not guarantee that the explanation is true. And the more satisfying the story, the more carefully it deserves to be examined.

Chapter Ten

Predictable Mistakes by Smart People

There is a comforting belief that intelligence protects us from error.

It does not. If anything, intelligence changes the style of the error. It makes the reasoning more elaborate, the explanations more convincing, the confidence more difficult to shake.But the underlying pattern remains the same.

Smart people do not make fewer mistakes. They make better-defended ones.

The Myth of Immunity

It's easy to assume that biases belong to other people.

The uninformed.The careless. The ones who haven't thought things through.But bias does not check credentials.

It operates quietly, efficiently, and without regard for how intelligent you are. In fact, the more capable you are at reasoning, the more material you have to work with when justifying a conclusion you've already reached.

You don't escape bias by thinking more.You often arm it.

Reasoning as a Tool, or a Weapon

Reasoning has two uses. It can be used to discover what is true. Or it can be used to defend what you already believe.

These are not the same activity.

In the first, you examine evidence, consider alternatives, and allow your conclusion to change. In the second, the conclusion is fixed. The reasoning is built around it.

The Inspector, ideally, is a neutral evaluator. But in practice, it is often handed a finished idea and asked to make it look respectable.

And because it is skilled, it does.

The Pattern of Predictable Error

As explored in *Predictably Irrational: The Hidden Forces That Shape Our Decisions* by Dan Ariely, our mistakes are not random. They follow patterns.

We overvalue what we already own. We are influenced by irrelevant comparisons. We respond differently depending on how choices are presented.

These patterns repeat across contexts, across individuals, across levels of intelligence. That's what makes them predictable.

And what makes them dangerous.

The Ownership Effect

One of the simplest examples:

You value something more once it belongs to you.

A mug you own feels worth more than the same mug sitting on a shelf. An idea you came up with feels stronger than an identical idea presented by someone else.

Ownership changes perception. It adds weight, importance, and a subtle resistance to letting go. This applies not just to objects, but to beliefs. Once an idea becomes yours, it becomes harder to question.

The Influence of Irrelevant Information

Consider how easily a number, any number, can shape your thinking.

An initial price. A suggested estimate. A random reference point.

Even when you know the number is arbitrary, it still exerts influence.

You adjust from it. You anchor to it. You carry it forward.

This is not a failure of knowledge. It is a feature of how the mind processes information.

Framing and Choice

Choices are not evaluated in isolation. They are evaluated in context.

Add a third option, and the original two change in appeal.

Present the same outcome differently, and preferences shift.

This is not because people are irrational in the usual sense It is because decisions are shaped by comparison, contrast, and presentation.

The Shortcutter does not analyze every option independently. It looks for the easiest way to decide. And the way choices are framed often provides that path.

The Intelligence Trap

Here's where things become more subtle.

When a less informed person makes a mistake, the error is often visible. When an intelligent person makes a mistake, the reasoning may be sophisticated enough to hide it.

They construct arguments. They draw connections. They anticipate objections. The result is a conclusion that feels solid, not because it is correct, but because it has been well defended.

This creates a trap.

The better you are at reasoning, the easier it becomes to convince yourself that your conclusion is justified.

Confidence Compounds the Problem

Confidence does not emerge from accuracy alone. It emerges from coherence.If an explanation fits together neatly, if the pieces align, if the reasoning flows, it feels right. And the more coherent the explanation, the more confident you become.

But coherence can be built on flawed assumptions. A structure can be internally consistent and still be wrong. And when confidence attaches itself to that structure, it becomes difficult to question.

A Familiar Scenario

You've likely experienced this. You form an opinion.You explain it clearly. You support it with examples. It feels solid.

Then someone asks a simple question–one you hadn't considered, and the structure shifts. Not dramatically. Just enough to reveal that something was missing.

The idea wasn't entirely wrong. But it wasn't as complete as it seemed.

The Role of Friction

The key to avoiding predictable mistakes is not intelligence.

It is friction. A pause. A question. A moment of resistance before accepting what feels obvious.

Friction interrupts the automatic process. It gives the Inspector time to arrive before the conclusion is finalized.

Without friction, thinking moves too quickly. And quick thinking, while efficient, is where these patterns thrive.

Practical Interruptions

When you feel confident in a conclusion, especially one that came easily, try introducing a small interruption:

- What would change my mind about this?
- What evidence would I accept if I disagreed with myself?
- Am I explaining, or am I defending?

These questions do not dismantle your thinking. They test its flexibility. And flexible thinking is more reliable than rigid confidence.

Back to the Workshop

In the workshop, this is the moment when a piece looks finished.

The lines are clean. The structure feels solid. Everything appears in order. But no one has tested it under real conditions.

No weight has been applied. No pressure has been introduced. It looks right. And because it looks right, it is often assumed to be right. Until it isn't.

What Comes Next

We've now seen how ideas are generated, shaped by bias, and reinforced through reasoning.

The next step is to examine how those ideas are expressed as arguments–and how they can go wrong in ways that are not just subtle, but systematic. Because when flawed thinking takes the form of structured reasoning, it becomes something more than a private mistake. It becomes a persuasive one.

For now, remember this:

Being smart does not protect you from error. It simply gives you better tools to explain it. And the more convincing your explanation, the more important it becomes to ask whether it's actually true.

Chapter Eleven

What a Good Argument Actually Looks Like

There comes a point in every workshop when someone steps back, wipes the sawdust off their hands, and says:

"Looks good."

This is not the same as being good.

Up to now, we've been generating ideas, watching them bend under bias, and noticing how easily they turn into convincing stories. Now we arrive at a different task entirely.

We stop admiring the piece. We start testing it.

From Opinion to Argument

An opinion is easy.

- "I think this works."
- "This seems right."
- "That doesn't make sense to me."

An argument is something else.

It's a structure. A claim supported by reasons. A conclusion that follows from what came before.

Not louder. Not longer. Just... built properly.

As laid out in A Rulebook for Arguments, a good argument isn't about winning. It's about whether the reasoning holds. And that depends on how it's constructed.

The Basic Frame

At its simplest, an argument has three parts:

- A claim – what you're saying is true
- Premises – the reasons or evidence supporting it
- A conclusion – what follows from those premises

Strip away the language, and you get something like this:

- Premise: All well-built chairs support weight
- Premise: This chair is well built
- Conclusion: This chair will support weight

It's not exciting. It's solid. And that's the point.

Validity vs Truth

Here's where things get interesting.

An argument can be valid without being true.

Validity means the structure works. If the premises are true, the conclusion follows. Truth means the premises actually reflect reality.

You can have a perfectly structured argument built on faulty assumptions:

- Premise: All birds can fly
- Premise: Penguins are birds
- Conclusion: Penguins can fly

The structure is sound. The conclusion follows. It just happens to be wrong. This distinction matters.

Because a well-structured argument can feel convincing even when its foundation is shaky.

The Inspector's Job

This is where the Inspector earns its keep. It doesn't care how confident the speaker is. It doesn't care how elegant the explanation sounds. It asks:

- Are the premises true?
- Do they support the conclusion?
- Is anything missing?

Not dramatic questions. But they have a way of exposing weak joints.

Common Structural Weaknesses

Most arguments don't fail loudly.

They fail quietly, in ways that are easy to overlook.

Missing Premises

The conclusion relies on something that was never stated.

"Of course this will work."

Based on what?

Unwarranted Assumptions

A premise is treated as true without evidence.

"People always respond this way."

Do they?

Leaps in Logic

The conclusion moves further than the premises allow.

"This happened, therefore this caused it."

Not necessarily. These aren't dramatic errors. They're small gaps.

But small gaps are where arguments collapse.

Clarity Over Cleverness

A good argument is not clever. It's clear.

It doesn't rely on rhetorical flourish or complicated phrasing. It doesn't hide behind jargon or stretch for effect. It says what it means, directly. And because of that, it can be examined.

Clever arguments, on the other hand, often distract from their own structure. They impress. They persuade. They move quickly.

But when you slow them down and look closely, you may find that the pieces don't quite connect.

Testing an Argment

You don't need formal training to evaluate an argument.

You need patience. Take a claim and ask:

1. What is being asserted?
2. What reasons are given?
3. Do those reasons actually support the claim?

Then go one step further:

- What would weaken this argument?
- What evidence would contradict it?

If an argument cannot survive these questions, it was never as strong as it seemed.

Agreement Is Not Proof

One of the more misleading signals of a good argument is agreement. If people nod, if the idea spreads, if it feels accepted, it begins to carry weight.

But agreement is social. Validity is structural.

A widely accepted argument can still be flawed. A correct argument can still be unpopular. The workshop doesn't care how many people like the chair. It cares whether it holds when someone sits down.

The Discipline of Slowing Down

Most poor arguments share one trait:

They move too quickly. From premise to conclusion.From idea to certainty.

Good reasoning introduces a pause.

A moment to examine. A moment to question. A moment to see whether the structure holds before moving on.

This pause is not hesitation. It is discipline.

A Familiar Exchange

You've likely heard something like this:

"This approach worked before, so it will work again."

It sounds reasonable. But examine it:

- Premise: It worked before
- Conclusion: It will work again

What's missing?

The assumption that the conditions are the same. If they aren't, the argument weakens.Not because the idea is impossible, but because the reasoning skipped a step.

Back to the Workshop

In the workshop, this is the stage where the piece is tested.

Not admired. Not explained. Tested.

- Does it hold weight?
- Does it function as intended?
- Do the joints stay firm under pressure?

You don't evaluate a chair by how well someone describes it. You evaluate it by whether it works.

What Comes Next

Now that we've looked at how arguments should be built, we turn to how they often go wrong. Because flawed reasoning doesn't always look flawed. It has patterns. Names. Familiar shapes that appear again and again.

Straw man. False cause. Slippery slope.

They sound technical. But you've seen them before.

In the next chapter, we'll walk through these patterns–not as abstract concepts, but as the common ways thinking quietly slips.

For now, remember this:

A good argument doesn't demand agreement. It earns it. And the only way to know the difference is to look at how it's built.

Chapter Twelve

The Museum of Bad Reasoning

If good arguments are well-built chairs, bad arguments are the ones that look fine until you sit down.

They have shape. They have polish. They sometimes even have confidence. What they lack is structure. And because they often sound reasonable, they pass inspection–until someone leans on them.

Welcome, then, to the museum.

Not a gallery of rare mistakes, but a collection of the most common exhibits. The ones you've seen before. The ones you've probably used yourself. The ones that appear so often they've earned names.

As illustrated in An Illustrated Book of Bad Arguments, these are not obscure errors. They are the standard ways reasoning goes quietly wrong.

Exhibit A:
The Straw Man

This one is popular because it's easy.

Instead of addressing the actual argument, you replace it with a weaker version–something easier to knock down.

Original: "We should consider adjusting the policy."

Response: "So you want to get rid of the policy entirely?"

Now you argue against the exaggerated version. It feels like engagement. It isn't. It's construction, building a version of the argument that was never made, then defeating it.

The structure looks active. The reasoning never touched the original point.

Exhibit B:
Ad Hominem

Latin for "to the person," which is where this argument goes immediately.

Instead of addressing the claim, you address the speaker.

- "You would say that."
- "What do you know about this?"
- "You're biased."

All of which may be true. None of which answer the argument.

A flawed person can make a valid point. A credible person can make a weak one. When the focus shifts from the idea to the individual, the structure collapses–just quietly enough that it often goes unnoticed.

Exhibit C:
False Cause

Two things happen close together, and the mind connects them.

This happened. Then that happened. Therefore, this caused that.

It feels logical. But sequence is not causation.

Just because one event follows another does not mean it produced it. There may be other factors. Hidden variables. Coincidence.

The story fits. The connection may not.

Exhibit D:
Slippery Slope

This one begins with a small step and ends in catastrophe.

"If we allow this, then that will happen, and eventually everything will fall apart."

Sometimes it's true.Often, it's speculation presented as inevitability.

The argument skips over the middle–those inconvenient steps where things might stop, change, or simply not unfold as predicted.

It moves quickly from possibility to certainty. And in doing so, it bypasses evidence entirely.

Exhibit E:
The False Dilemma

Two options are presented.

One is undesirable. The other is preferred. And you are told these are the only choices.

- "We can do this, or we can fail."
- "You're either with this approach, or against progress."

It simplifies the landscape. But in doing so, it removes everything in between. Most real situations contain more than two options. The false dilemma trims them away, leaving a cleaner–but less accurate–picture.

Exhibit F:
Circular Reasoning

This argument is self-supporting. The conclusion appears in the premise.

- "This works because it's effective."
- "We know this is true because it's correct."

It feels like explanation. It's repetition. The structure moves in a circle–never expanding, never adding support, just restating the claim in slightly different language.

Exhibit G:
Hasty Generalization

A small sample becomes a broad conclusion. You meet two difficult clients and conclude that all clients are difficult. You see a few examples and assume they represent the whole.

This is pattern-making at speed.It ignores scale, variation, and the possibility that what you've seen is not enough to justify what you believe. The conclusion feels reasonable. The evidence is thin.

Why These Work

Each of these fallacies shares a common trait:

They simplify. They reduce complexity. They move quickly. They feel complete. And because they align with the Shortcutter's preferences–speed, clarity, efficiency–they are accepted without much resistance.

They don't announce themselves as errors. They present themselves as conclusions.

The Danger of Familiarity

Once you've seen these patterns, you'll notice something. They are everywhere. In conversations. In headlines. In arguments that sound persuasive until you slow them down. And that familiarity creates a risk.

You begin to recognize them in others–quickly, confidently. But the more important task is recognizing them in your own thinking.

Which is harder.Because your own arguments feel reasonable from the inside.

A Practical Approach

When you encounter an argument, especially one that feels convincing, try a simple test :

- What is the actual claim?
- What evidence supports it?
- Does the reasoning follow, or does it jump?

Then look for the pattern:

- Is the argument misrepresenting something?
- Is it attacking the person instead of the idea?
- Is it assuming cause without proof?

You don't need to name the fallacy. You just need to notice the gap.

Back to the Workshop

In the workshop, these fallacies are the shortcuts that look like craftsmanship.

A joint that's glued but not fitted. A support that appears solid but hasn't been tested. A design that assumes more than it proves.

From a distance, everything looks fine. Up close, the weaknesses show.

What Comes Next

We've now seen how arguments should be built–and how they often fail.

Next, we connect the two threads. Because these fallacies don't appear out of nowhere. They are built from the same biases we explored earlier.

Confirmation bias leads to selective arguments. Pattern-seeking leads to false cause. Narrative thinking leads to oversimplification.

In the next chapter, we'll bring these pieces together.

For now, remember this:

Bad reasoning rarely looks bad at first glance. It looks efficient. It looks convincing. And that's exactly why it needs to be examined.

Chapter Thirteen

How Bias Becomes Fallacy

By now, you've seen both sides of the operation.

On one side, the Shortcutter–quietly shaping what you notice, what you remember, what feels true. On the other, the Inspector–building arguments, testing structure, asking whether things hold.

In theory, these are separate steps. In practice, they overlap. And when they do, something interesting happens:

Bias doesn't stay in the background. It steps forward and becomes reasoning. That's where fallacies are born.

From Bend to Structure

A bias is a bend in thinking. It tilts your attention It favors certain information. It nudges you toward particular conclusions.

A fallacy is what happens when that bend is built into an argument.

It's no longer just a tendency. It's a structure. And once it becomes structure, it can be shared, defended, and repeated.

The Invisible Transition

The transition from bias to fallacy is easy to miss.

It doesn't feel like a shift. You notice certain evidence. You form a conclusion. You explain that conclusion. At no point does anything feel broken.

But underneath, the process has been shaped by preference rather than proof. The argument reflects not just the facts, but the way those facts were selected, interpreted, and arranged.

Confirmation Bias & Cherry-Picked Arguments

Start with confirmation bias. You favor information that supports your view. You overlook what doesn't.

Then you build an argument.

The result is a case that appears well-supported, but only because it includes the evidence you chose to include. Contradictions are absent. Alternatives are missing.

The fallacy isn't in the structure alone. It's in what the structure leaves out.

Availability & Hasty Generalization

What comes to mind easily feels important. You recall vivid examples. You treat them as representative. Then you argue from them.

"Everyone is doing this."

"This always happens."

The leap from a few memorable cases to a general rule feels natural. But the argument rests on limited evidence, expanded into something broader than it can support.

Anchoring & Distorted Judgments

An initial number sets the stage. You adjust from it, even when it's arbitrary. Then you justify your position.

The argument appears reasoned. It includes comparisons, estimates, conclusions. But all of it is built around a starting point that may have had no basis at all. The anchor doesn't appear in the argument.

Its influence does.

Narrative Bias & False Cause

You arrange events into a story. This led to that. This happened because of that. Then you present the explanation.

The argument flows. It makes sense. It feels complete. But the connection between events may be assumed rather than demonstrated.

The story supplies the cause. The argument presents it as fact.

Pattern-Seeking & Slippery Logic

You detect a pattern. A small change appears to lead toward a larger outcome. Then you extend it.

"If this happens, then that will follow, and eventually..."

The argument builds a chain. Each link seems plausible. The full sequence feels inevitable. But the connections between links are rarely tested.

Possibility becomes certainty–one step at a time.

The Illusion of Sound Reasoning

Here's the problem. Once bias becomes fallacy, the reasoning doesn't look obviously flawed.

It has structure. It has flow. It often has confidence. It resembles good thinking. And that resemblance is enough to carry it forward.

People agree. The argument spreads. The conclusion settles in. Not because it has been fully tested, but because it has been well presented.

Why This Matters

It's one thing to hold a biased belief. It's another to build that belief into an argument that persuades others–and reinforces itself.

Once an idea is expressed as reasoning, it becomes harder to challenge. It feels more solid. More complete. More justified. But if the underlying bias remains unexamined, the structure rests on uneven ground.

Breaking the Chain

To interrupt this process, you don't start with the argument.

You start with the input.

Ask:

- What information did I include–and what did I leave out?
- What assumptions shaped this conclusion?
- What would this look like from a different perspective?

Then examine the structure:

- Does the conclusion follow from the evidence?
- Are there steps that feel obvious but haven't been tested?

This is not about dismantling every argument. It's about making sure the foundation is visible before trusting the structure.

A Familiar Moment

You're in a conversation.

An argument is presented–clear, confident, persuasive.

It feels right. Then, a question:

"What about this?"

A piece of information that doesn't fit. The argument shifts. Not because it was entirely wrong, but because it was incomplete.

The bias shaped what was included. The fallacy shaped how it was presented.

Back to the Workshop

In the workshop, this is the difference between a flaw in the material and a flaw in the construction.

A warped board might go unnoticed at first. But once it's built into the frame, the entire structure leans. The problem isn't just the board anymore.

It's the way it was used. Bias is the warp.

Fallacy is the structure built on it.

What Comes Next

We've now connected the pieces.

Ideas are generated. They are shaped by bias. They are expressed through reasoning–sometimes well, sometimes poorly.

Now we turn to something more practical. How do you manage this process?

How do you move from generation, through distortion, into testing–and back again?

In the next section, we step out of theory and into method.

For now, remember this:

You don't just think. You build arguments from what you think. And if the input is tilted,the structure will lean, no matter how carefully it's assembled.

Chapter Fourteen

The Thinking Loop

At some point, you stop asking how thinking ought to work and start asking how to make it work on purpose. Up to now, we've taken the workshop apart.

We've watched the Inventor scatter ideas across the bench.

We've seen the Shortcutter shape them–quickly, sometimes carelessly.

We've invited the Inspector in to test what survives.

Now it's time to put the place back together. Not as a theory. As a process.

From Pieces to Process

Most thinking feels like a single act.

You have a thought. You follow it. You arrive somewhere. But as you've seen, that's not what's happening.

Thinking is a sequence.

Generate/ Distort/ Test/ Refine

It's not a straight line. It's a loop.And the quality of your thinking depends less on where you start than on how many times you move through that loop–properly.

Stage One:
Generate *(Let the Inventor Work)*

This is where ideas are born.

Messy. Incomplete. Sometimes promising, often not. The mistake most people make here is trying to be right too soon. They filter ideas as they appear. They judge them prematurely. They aim for correctness instead of possibility.

The result is predictable thinking. Fewer ideas. Safer ideas. Familiar ideas. A workshop that produces the same chair every time.

Good thinking begins with volume. Not endless, but sufficient. Enough ideas to give yourself options. Enough variation to avoid being trapped by the first answer that feels right.

At this stage, the rule is simple: Do not evaluate. Just produce.

Stage Two:
Distort *(Recognize the Shortcutter)*

Whether you notice it or not, this happens automatically.

Ideas are shaped by bias.Some feel right immediately. Others are dismissed just as quickly. Certain details stand out. Others fade.

You don't choose this stage. But you can become aware of it.

This is where most thinking quietly goes off course, not because of bad intent, but because of unnoticed influence. So instead of trying to eliminate distortion, you do something more practical:

You observe it.

- Why does this idea feel right?
- What assumptions am I making?
- What might I be overlooking?

You're not correcting yet. You're noticing the bend before it becomes the structure.

Stage Three:
Test *(Call in the Inspector)*

Now the work becomes deliberate. This is where you slow down. You take the ideas that survived the first two stages and examine them.

Not harshly. Not cynically. Carefully.

- What is the claim?
- What supports it?
- Does the reasoning hold?
- What would challenge it?

This is where many ideas fall apart. That's not failure. That's filtration. A weak idea exposed early is a problem avoided later.

Stage Four:
Refine *(Back to the Bench)*

After testing, something remains.

Not always the original idea. Often a revised version–stronger, clearer, more grounded.

This is refinement. You adjust. You combine. You rebuild. Then, if you're doing it right, you loop again.

Generate new variations. Notice new distortions. Test again.

Each pass improves the structure. Not dramatically. Incrementally.

Why the Loop Matters

Most poor thinking fails not because of one bad step, but because the loop is broken.

- Ideas are generated and accepted without testing
- Bias shapes conclusions without being noticed
- Arguments are formed without revision

The process stops too early. The first idea becomes the final answer. The first explanation becomes the accepted truth. The loop never closes.

The Discipline of Iteration

Good thinking is iterative.

It revisits. It revises. It resists the urge to settle too quickly.

This requires patience. And patience is not a trait the mind naturally favors.

The Shortcutter wants closure.

The Inventor wants novelty.

The Inspector wants certainty.

The loop requires something else: Willingness to stay in the process.

A Practical Example

Consider a simple decision: choosing a direction for a project.

Generate:

List multiple approaches–some conventional, some not.

Distort (observe):

Notice which options feel appealing and why. Familiarity? Simplicity? Prior success?

Test:

Examine each option. What assumptions does it rely on? What risks are present? What evidence supports it?

Refine:

Combine elements. Adjust the approach. Strengthen weak points.

Then, if needed–repeat. Not endlessly. But enough to move beyond the obvious.

When to Stop

A fair question. If thinking is a loop, when do you exit?

The answer is not perfection. It's sufficiency.

You stop when:

- The idea has been tested under reasonable conditions
- The major assumptions have been examined
- The structure holds under pressure

Not because it cannot be improved, but because further refinement yields diminishing returns.

At some point, the work must leave the workshop.

Common Breakdowns

Watch for these:

Skipping Generation

Settling for the first idea.

Ignoring Distortion

Assuming your thinking is neutral.

Avoiding Testing

Preferring confidence over examination.

Neglecting Refinement

Treating ideas as finished too early.

Each one interrupts the loop. Each one reduces the quality of the result.

Back to the Workshop

In the workshop, the loop is the rhythm of the place.

Build. Check. Adjust. Repeat.

The best work doesn't emerge in a single pass. It emerges through iteration–small improvements layered over time. The difference between something that works and something that holds is often just one more pass through the loop.

What Comes Next

Now that the process is clear, the next question is practical:

When do you lean into creativity?

When do you slow down?

When do you question, and when do you move forward?

In the next chapter, we'll look at timing–how to use each part of the workshop at the right moment.

Because knowing the loop is one thing. Running it well is another.

For now, remember this:

Thinking is not a single act.

It's a cycle.And the more deliberately you move through it, the less you'll have to rely on whatever happened to come first.

Chapter Fifteen

When to Trust Each Voice

By now, you know the crew.

The Inventor generates. The Shortcutter simplifies. The Inspector tests.

Individually, each is useful. Collectively, they are powerful. But only if you let them speak at the right time. Because most thinking problems are not caused by the wrong voice. They're caused by the right voice showing up at the wrong moment.

The Timing Problem

Imagine trying to build something while being inspected at every step.

You sketch an idea. Someone interrupts: "Does that hold up?"

You try a variation. Another interruption: "What's your evidence?"

Before long, you stop sketching. That's what happens when the Inspector arrives too early.

Now imagine the opposite.

You build freely. You assemble quickly. No one checks anything.

The result may look impressive. Until it's used.

That's what happens when the Inspector arrives too late, or not at all. Good thinking isn't just about what you do.

It's about when you do it.

The Natural Disorder

Left to its own devices, the mind doesn't follow a clean sequence.

The Shortcutter jumps in immediately. The Inventor follows, building around the first idea.

The Inspector is either ignored or recruited to defend what's already been decided.

The process is out of order. And when the order is wrong, even good thinking tools produce poor results.

Stage One: Let the Inventor Speak First

At the beginning, you need possibilities.

This is not the time for precision. It's not the time for judgment.

It's the time to ask:

- What are the options?
- What haven't I considered?
- What if the obvious answer isn't the only one?

The Inventor thrives here. It explores. It connects. It produces. Your job is not to control it too tightly. Your job is to keep it moving.

If you interrupt too early–if you demand correctness before generation–you will narrow your thinking before it has a chance to expand. And once narrowed, it rarely widens again.

Stage Two: Keep the Shortcutter in Check

The Shortcutter doesn't wait its turn.

It arrives immediately, offering conclusions that feel right. This is useful in routine situations. It is dangerous in complex ones. So instead of trusting or rejecting it entirely, you manage it.

You notice:

- Which ideas feel obvious
- Which conclusions arrive quickly
- Which options seem immediately appealing

Then you ask:

Why?

Not to eliminate the instinct–just to understand it.

The Shortcutter provides signals. But those signals are not final answers.

Stage Three: Invite the Inspector–Deliberately

At some point, the tone must change.

You move from exploration to evaluation. This is where the Inspector belongs. Not earlier. Not indefinitely delayed. Right here.

Now you ask:

- Does this idea hold up?
- What assumptions am I making?
- What evidence supports this?
- What would challenge it?

The Inspector slows the process down. That's its job. It introduces friction where speed would otherwise carry you past important details.

Stage Four: Don't Let the Inspector Take Over

There is a temptation, once the Inspector is engaged, to let it dominate.

Everything becomes analysis. Every idea is scrutinized immediately. Nothing moves forward without exhaustive proof.

This creates a different problem. Paralysis.

Thinking becomes so careful that it stops producing anything new. The workshop turns into a testing facility with nothing left to test.

So you limit the Inspector's role. It evaluates. It does not prevent generation.

A Simple Sequence

In practice, the order looks like this:

1. Inventor – generate freely
2. Shortcutter – notice reactions, don't trust them blindly
3. Inspector – test deliberately
4. Inventor (again) – refine and rebuild

Then repeat as needed. Not rigidly. But intentionally.

A Familiar Misstep

Consider a common situation: writing.

You begin with an idea. Immediately, the Inspector appears:

> "This isn't quite right."
>
> "That doesn't make sense."
>
> "This needs to be better."

So you stop. The idea never develops.

Now consider the opposite.

You write freely. You follow the idea wherever it goes. You never step back to evaluate.

The result is volume without clarity. In both cases, the issue isn't ability. It's timing.

Trust vs Control

The goal is not to eliminate any voice. It's to trust each one appropriately.

- Trust the Inventor to explore
- Trust the Shortcutter to signal–but not decide
- Trust the Inspector to evaluate–but not dominate

Each has a role. Each becomes a problem when it steps outside that role.

Signals You're Out of Order

You can often tell when the timing is off.

- If you have no new ideas = the Inspector is too early
- If everything feels obvious = the Shortcutter is unchecked
- If nothing gets finished = the Inspector is too dominant
- If everything feels scattered = the Inventor is unbounded

These aren't failures. They're indicators.

Back to the Workshop

In the workshop, timing is everything.

- You don't sand before you cut.
- You don't test before you build.
- You don't finish before you've shaped the piece.

Each step has its place.

Out of order, even good work becomes difficult. In order, the process flows.

What Comes Next

Now that you know how to sequence the voices, the next step is applying this in the real world.

Not in controlled examples. In situations where time is limited, information is incomplete, and the pressure to decide is real.

Writing.

Teaching.

Leadership.

Everyday decisions.

In the next chapter, we bring the workshop out into the world.

For now, remember this:

The problem is not that your mind has too many voices. The problem is letting the wrong one lead at the wrong time. And once you learn the order, thinking becomes less about reacting and more about directing.

Chapter Sixteen

Thinking Where It Actually Matters

Up to now, the workshop has been tidy.

Controlled examples. Clean sequences. Enough time to notice what's happening before something else interrupts.

That's not how thinking usually works.

Out in the world, you don't get a quiet bench and a full set of tools laid out in order. You get noise. Deadlines. Incomplete information. People who are confident, people who are wrong, and occasionally people who are both.

And somewhere in the middle of that, you're expected to think clearly.

The Conditions Are Never Ideal

- You are asked to decide before you have all the facts.
- You are asked to explain before you've fully understood.
- You are asked to move forward while parts of the structure are still uncertain.

In those conditions, the Shortcutter becomes very persuasive.

It offers speed. It offers closure. It offers the comfort of an answer.

The Inventor may offer ideas, but they take time. The Inspector may offer caution, but it slows things down. So the temptation is clear:

Take the answer that arrives first. Explain it well. Move on. And most of the time, that's exactly what happens.

The Real Work of Thinking

Thinking matters most in the moments where the cost of being wrong is not immediately obvious.

Writing something that will be read later.
Teaching something that will shape understanding.
Making a decision that will unfold over time.

These are not moments where speed alone is enough.

They require something else:

Deliberate thinking under imperfect conditions.

Thinking in Writing

Writing exposes your thinking.

An idea that feels clear in your head often changes when you try to put it into words. Gaps appear. Assumptions become visible. Connections that seemed obvious begin to weaken.

This is not a failure of writing. It's a revelation of thinking.

The process works like this:

- The Inventor generates the initial idea
- The Shortcutter shapes it into something that feels coherent
- The act of writing invites the Inspector to examine it

If you skip the last step, the writing may sound confident–but it may not hold. If you invite the Inspector too early, the writing never develops.

Good writing follows the loop:

Draft. Question. Revise. Not once. Repeatedly.

Thinking in Teaching

Teaching is thinking made visible to others.

You're not just presenting conclusions. You're modeling how those conclusions were reached. And students are quick to pick up on shortcuts.

If the explanation jumps, they learn to jump. If the reasoning skips steps, they assume the steps aren't necessary.

The challenge is balance. Too much Inventor, and the lesson becomes scattered.

Too much Inspector, and it becomes rigid and inaccessible.

The goal is clarity without oversimplification. To show structure without removing complexity entirely. Because teaching is not just about delivering answers.

It's about shaping how others think.

Thinking in Decisions

Decisions rarely arrive with complete information.

You don't get a full set of data neatly organized and labeled.

You get fragments. Time pressure. Partial evidence. Conflicting perspectives.

Under these conditions, the Shortcutter becomes dominant.

It fills in gaps. It favors familiarity. It pushes toward resolution.

This is not always wrong. But it is often unexamined. So the goal is not to eliminate speed. It's to introduce just enough friction to improve the outcome. A pause. A question:

- What am I assuming?
- What don't I know?
- What would change this decision?

You don't stop the process. You interrupt it–briefly. And that interruption is often enough to prevent predictable mistakes.

Thinking with Other People

Thinking alone is one thing. Thinking with others is something else entirely. Now you're dealing with:

- Different assumptions
- Different experiences
- Different levels of confidence

And often, different conclusions.

This introduces a new challenge:

Agreement can feel like validation. Disagreement can feel like error. But neither is necessarily true.

In group settings, the risk is that reasoning becomes performance. Ideas are defended rather than examined. Positions are maintained rather than tested.

The Inspector, instead of evaluating ideas, begins to defend them.

The result is not better thinking. It's stronger disagreement.

A Better Approach

When thinking with others, the goal shifts.

Not to win. Not to persuade immediately. But to understand the structure of the ideas being presented. Ask:

- What is the claim?
- What supports it?
- Where might it be incomplete?

These questions move the conversation away from positions and toward reasoning. And reasoning, unlike opinion, can be examined.

The Pressure to Appear Certain

One of the quiet pressures in real-world thinking is the expectation of certainty.

You're expected to have answers. To sound confident. To move forward without hesitation. But certainty is often a performance.

It's what happens when the Shortcutter and the Inspector align.Not in search of truth, but in presentation.

The conclusion is delivered. The reasoning is polished. The uncertainty is hidden. This can be effective. It can also be misleading.

Because the appearance of certainty is not the same as the presence of sound thinking.

Allowing for Uncertainty

There is a different approach.

One that feels less comfortable at first. You allow for uncertainty. You acknowledge what is known. You recognize what is not. You remain open to revision.

This is not indecision. It is accuracy. And in many cases, it leads to better outcomes–not because it avoids error entirely, but because it reduces the cost of being wrong.

Back to the Workshop

In the workshop, this is where the work leaves the bench.

The piece is used. Not in perfect conditions. Not under controlled circumstances. In the real world.

> Where weight is uneven.
>
> Where pressure is unpredictable.
>
> Where small flaws become visible.

And what holds is not what looked best on the table. It's what was built carefully enough to handle reality.

What Comes Next

We've now moved from understanding thinking to applying it.

The next step is practical. Tools.

Not abstract ideas, but specific methods you can use immediately, to generate better ideas, interrupt bias, and test reasoning. Because understanding the workshop is useful. But having the right tools within reach is what makes the work possible.

For now, remember this:

Thinking matters most when it's hardest to do well. And those are exactly the moments when it's worth slowing down just enough to get it right.

Chapter Seventeen

Creative Tools That Actually Work

Every workshop eventually reaches this point.

Enough theory. Enough discussion about how things should be done. You want tools.

Not philosophical ones. Not decorative ones. The kind you can pick up, use, and see whether they actually improve the work.

This chapter is a small drawer of such tools. Not exhaustive. Not complicated. Just reliable ways to help the Inventor do its job without wandering off into the weeds.

A Note Before We Begin

Creative tools are not magic. They don't guarantee good ideas. They don't replace effort. They don't make thinking easy.

What they do is simple:

They change the conditions under which thinking happens. And when you change the conditions, different ideas appear.

Tool 1:
The "Ten Ideas" Rule

Give yourself a problem. Now generate ten possible solutions.

Not three. Not five. Ten.

The first few will be obvious. Familiar. Reasonable.

Then something happens. You run out of easy answers. And when that happens, the Inventor is forced to look elsewhere–to stretch, to combine, to try something less predictable.

The goal isn't that all ten are good. It's that the last few are different.

Tool 2:
Reverse the Problem

Instead of asking how to solve the problem, ask:

"How would I make this worse?"

Be specific.

- How would I guarantee failure?
- What would create the exact opposite of what I want?

Then examine those answers. They often reveal hidden assumptions, overlooked factors, and points of weakness. Once you see how something fails, you understand more clearly how it might succeed.

Tool 3:
Change the Frame

Describe the problem in a completely different way.

A business problem becomes a design problem.

A teaching challenge becomes a storytelling problem.

A logistical issue becomes a behavioral one.

Each frame brings its own set of tools. If you stay in one frame, you get one kind of answer. Change the frame, and the problem changes shape.

Tool 4:
Forced Connection

Take two unrelated things. A concept from your field. Something entirely outside it. Now ask:

"How could these connect?"

Most attempts will fail. That's fine.

The goal is not immediate usefulness. It's movement.

You are nudging the Inventor away from familiar patterns, forcing it to build something it wouldn't normally consider.Occasionally, something sticks. And when it does, it often leads somewhere new.

Tool 5:
Add a Constraint

This one feels backward. You don't remove limitations. You add them.

- Solve the problem using only half the resources
- Explain the idea in one paragraph
- Design the solution without using the usual method

Constraints force creativity. They remove the obvious path and require the Inventor to find another.

Without constraints, thinking can become vague. With constraints, it becomes specific.

Tool 6:
The "What If" Ladder

Start with the current situation.

Now ask:

"What if this were different?"

Then build:

- What if time were limited?
- What if resources were unlimited?
- What if the goal changed?
- What if the constraints disappeared?

Each question shifts the conditions. Each shift produces a new set of possibilities. You're not committing to these changes.

You're exploring them.

Tool 7:
Delay Judgment *(Deliberately)*

This is less a tool and more a discipline.

When generating ideas, do not evaluate them immediately.

Not silently. Not subtly. Not at all.

The moment you begin judging ideas as they appear, the Inventor slows down. It becomes cautious. It produces less.

So you separate the stages:

First, generate. Later, evaluate. Not both at once.

Tool 8:
Borrow a Perspective

Ask:

"How would someone else approach this?"

A different profession. A different field. A different level of experience.

- How would an engineer solve this?
- How would a storyteller approach it?
- How would a beginner see it?

Perspective changes the tools you reach for. And sometimes, the right tool is simply one you hadn't considered.

Tool 9:
Make It Smaller

Large problems can stall thinking. They feel too complex, too broad. So you reduce them.

> What is the smallest version of this problem?
>
> What is one part I can solve?

Once you solve a smaller piece, momentum builds. And momentum is often what the Inventor needs to keep moving.

Tool 10:
Walk Away

This one feels unproductive. It isn't. When you stop actively working on a problem, the Inventor doesn't stop. It continues quietly–connecting, sorting, recombining.

You've experienced this:

The solution appears later. Unexpectedly. Without effort.

That's not luck. That's delayed processing.

Sometimes the best way to move forward is to step away long enough for the pieces to settle.

Choosing the Right Tool

You don't need all of these at once. You need one or two, applied deliberately. The choice depends on where you're stuck:

- No ideas? Generate more *(Ten Ideas, What If)*
- Same ideas? Break patterns *(Forced Connection, Change Frame)*
- Too vague? Add structure *(Constraints, Make It Smaller)*
- Stuck entirely? Step away

Each tool addresses a different problem.

What These Tools Have in Common

They all do one thing: They interrupt the obvious.

They prevent the first idea from becoming the only idea.

They create space, just enough for something different to appear.

Back to the Workshop

In the workshop, tools are not admired. They are used.

You don't debate whether a hammer is philosophically sound. You pick it up and see if it works.

Creative tools are the same. They are practical. Some will suit you. Some won't.

The point is not to adopt all of them. The point is to have something within reach when thinking stalls.

What Comes Next

Generating ideas is only part of the process.

Next, we turn to the other side of the work:

How to catch yourself when your thinking begins to bend, and how to interrupt bias before it turns into error.

Because good ideas are only useful if they survive what comes next.

For now, remember this:

Creativity is not waiting for inspiration. It's creating the conditions where different ideas have a chance to appear.

Chapter Eighteen

Catching Yourself in the Act

Most thinking errors share a common feature:

You don't notice them while they're happening.

You notice them later–after the decision, after the argument, after the email has been sent and the moment has passed. At that point, the Inspector arrives with perfect clarity and excellent timing… for yesterday.

This chapter is about something more difficult and more useful:

Catching the error while it's still in motion. Not perfectly. Not every time. But often enough to change the outcome.

Why This Is Hard

Bias operates quickly. It doesn't announce itself. It doesn't ask permission. It produces conclusions that feel natural, immediate, and correct. And because those conclusions feel right, there's no obvious reason to question them.

The mind moves on.

By the time doubt appears, the thinking is already complete. So the challenge is not knowledge. You already know about bias.

The challenge is timing.

From Awareness to Interruption

Knowing about bias is like knowing that roads can be slippery.

It helps. But it doesn't prevent you from sliding.

What matters is what you do in the moment–when the conditions are right for error.

That requires a shift:

From understanding bias, to interrupting it.

The Signals

Bias doesn't arrive with a label, but it does leave traces.

Certain patterns tend to show up when your thinking is being shaped too quickly or too narrowly.

Watch for these:

- A conclusion that arrives immediately
- A strong feeling of certainty with little evidence
- A reaction that aligns perfectly with what you already believe
- A sense that the answer is obvious and doesn't require further thought

None of these guarantee error. But they are signals. They suggest that the Shortcutter may be moving too quickly.

The Pause

The simplest intervention is also the most effective:

A pause. Not a long one. Not a dramatic one. Just enough to create a gap between the thought and the acceptance of it.

In that gap, something changes. The automatic process slows.

The Inspector has time to arrive. The conclusion becomes something you can examine rather than simply accept.

The Questions That Interrupt

The pause needs direction.

Otherwise, the mind simply continues along the same path.

So you give it a small set of questions–simple enough to use, strong enough to matter.

- What am I assuming?
- What don't I know?
- Why does this feel right?
- What would I think if I disagreed with this?

These are not complicated. They don't require deep analysis.

They just shift the thinking from automatic to deliberate.

Catching Specific Patterns

Different biases require different interruptions.

You don't need to identify them by name. You just need to recognize their shape.

When you're only seeing one side, ask:

What am I not seeing?

When something feels common or important, ask:

Is this actually frequent, or just memorable?

When a number or comparison stands out, ask:

Why this number? What would I think without it?

When a story feels complete, ask:

What might be missing?

Each question introduces friction. And friction is what slows bias down.

The Cost of Not Interrupting

When you don't interrupt, the process continues unchecked.

The conclusion forms.

The reasoning follows.

The confidence grows.

By the time you revisit the idea, it has structure. And structured ideas are harder to change. Not because they are correct, but because they are established.

A Small Example

You read a headline. It confirms something you already believe. You nod. You move on.

Now insert a pause.

- What is the source?
- What information is missing?
- Would I react the same way if this said the opposite?

Nothing dramatic. But the thinking shifts. The conclusion is no longer automatic.

Making It Habitual

Catching yourself once is useful. Catching yourself regularly is transformative. But it requires practice.

Not formal practice. Repeated, small interventions.

- A pause before agreeing
- A question before concluding
- A moment of doubt before certainty

Over time, these become habits. And habits, once formed, operate with the same efficiency as bias, but in your favor.

The Balance

There is a risk here.

Too much interruption, and thinking becomes slow, hesitant, overanalyzed. Too little, and it becomes automatic, unexamined, predictable.

The goal is not constant scrutiny. It's selective interruption. You don't question everything. You question the things that matter,, or the things that feel too easy.

Back to the Workshop

In the workshop, this is the moment before a cut is made.

You've measured. You've aligned. You're about to act. And then, just briefly, you check. Not because you expect an error.

But because correcting it now is easier than fixing it later.

What Comes Next

We've now seen how to generate ideas and how to interrupt bias as it appears. The next step is testing–systematically, consistently.

Not just asking questions in the moment, but applying a framework that ensures your thinking holds under pressure. Because catching yourself is one skill. Knowing how to evaluate what remains is another.

For now, remember this:

You won't eliminate bias. But you can catch it–mid-thought, mid-decision, mid-argument, if you learn to pause just long enough to see what's happening.

Chapter Nineteen

The Argument Checklist

There comes a moment in every piece of thinking when the question changes. You're no longer asking, What do I think?

You're asking, Does this hold up?

This is where the workshop gets quiet. No new materials. No fresh ideas scattered across the bench. Just what's already been built, sitting there, waiting to be tested. And for that, you need something simple.

Not a theory. Not a lecture. A checklist.

Why a Checklist?

Because thinking is slippery.

Even when you know what to look for, it's easy to miss something. A gap in reasoning. An assumption that went unexamined. A conclusion that arrived a little too quickly.

A checklist does one thing well:

It slows you down just enough to notice what you might otherwise overlook. Not dramatically. Just deliberately.

The Five-Part Check

You don't need fifty questions. You need a handful that cover the structure. Here they are.

1. What is the claim?

Start here.

What, exactly, is being said?

Not implied. Not suggested. Stated.

If you can't clearly identify the claim, you can't evaluate the argument. This is where many discussions go sideways, not because people disagree, but because they're not actually addressing the same point. Clarity first.

2. What supports it?

Now look at the reasons.

> What evidence is being offered?
>
> What examples?
>
> What assumptions are doing the heavy lifting?

Strip away the language. What's left?

An argument without support is not an argument. It's a statement.

3. Does the reasoning follow?

This is the structural check.

> Do the premises actually lead to the conclusion?
>
> Or is there a jump?
>
> A quiet leap from "this is true" to "therefore, this must be true"?

This is where many arguments feel right but don't hold. The pieces are present. They just don't connect.

4. What's missing?

No argument includes everything. The question is whether what's left out matters.

- Are alternative explanations considered?
- Is contradictory evidence addressed?
- Are key assumptions left unstated?

Sometimes what's missing is more important than what's included.

5. What would change my mind?

This is the final–and often most revealing–question.

If the answer is "nothing," the argument isn't being evaluated.

It's being defended. A good argument allows for the possibility of revision. Not because it's weak, but because it's honest.

Using the Checklist in Practice

You don't need to announce it. You don't need to formalize it.

You just run through it, quietly, internally, consistently.

A conversation. An article. Your own thinking. The process is the same.

- What's the claim?
- What supports it?
- Does it follow?
- What's missing?
- What would change this?

Five questions. That's enough.

When the Checklist Feels Uncomfortable

There will be moments when applying this feels inconvenient.

The argument sounds good. The conclusion aligns with what you believe. Everything feels settled.

Then you ask the questions. And something shifts. A gap appears. An assumption becomes visible. A conclusion weakens.

This is not a problem. It's the process working.

The Checklist and Your Own Thinking

It's easy to apply this to others. It's more difficult, and more important, to apply it to yourself.

Your own arguments feel clear from the inside. They make sense. They fit together. Which is exactly why they need to be checked.

Run the same questions:

- What am I claiming?
- What supports it?
- Am I skipping steps?
- What am I leaving out?

You won't catch everything. But you'll catch more than you would have otherwise.

Avoiding Overuse

There is a temptation to turn this into a constant habit–questioning everything, examining every thought, slowing every decision.

That's not the goal. The checklist is a tool, not a lifestyle.

Use it where it matters:

- Important decisions
- Public arguments
- Claims that carry weight

Not every thought requires inspection. But the ones that do benefit from it.

A Familiar Example

Consider a simple claim:

"This approach will improve results."

Run the checklist.

- Claim: The approach improves results
- Support: What evidence is given? Past success? Assumptions?
- Reasoning: Does past success guarantee future results?
- Missing: Are conditions the same? Are alternatives considered?
- Revision: What would show this doesn't work?

The claim hasn't been dismissed. It's been examined. And that examination changes how you treat it.

Back to the Workshop

In the workshop, this is the final inspection.

Not a glance. A check.

> Are the joints aligned?
>
> Are the supports sound?
>
> Will this hold under pressure?

You don't assume. You verify. Because once the work leaves the shop, it meets reality. And reality is less forgiving than theory.

What Comes Next

You now have tools for generating ideas, interrupting bias, and testing reasoning.

The final step is something larger.

Not just how you think–but how thinking is used. Because reasoning is not neutral.

> It can clarify.
>
> It can persuade.
>
> It can also mislead.

In the next chapter, we turn to that question.

Not how thinking works, but what it's used for.

For now, remember this:

A good argument doesn't just sound right. It survives being questioned.

Chapter Twenty

Truth vs. Persuasion

There is a moment, usually subtle, when thinking changes its purpose. You're no longer asking, Is this true?

You're asking, Will this convince?

The difference is small on the surface. The consequences are not.

Two Different Aims

Truth and persuasion often travel together.

A clear, well-supported idea is easier to accept. A sound argument can be persuasive. But they are not the same goal.

Truth asks:

- What is accurate?
- What holds up under scrutiny?

Persuasion asks:

- What will people accept?
- What will move them?

Sometimes those answers align. Sometimes they don't.

When Persuasion Leads

In practice, persuasion often takes the lead. Not because people are dishonest. Because they are human.

You want your idea to land.

You want your argument to work.

You want the other person to agree.

So the presentation shifts. You emphasize what supports your case.

You simplify what complicates it.

You choose examples that resonate. None of this feels like manipulation. It feels like clarity.

The Quiet Slide

The transition is gradual.

You begin with an idea.

You shape it for communication.

You remove what seems unnecessary.

At some point, something changes. The goal is no longer accuracy.

It's impact. And impact has its own rules:

- Simpler is better
- Clearer is stronger
- More confident is more persuasive

Even when the reality is more complex.

The Tools of Persuasion

Persuasion has a familiar toolkit. You've seen it.

- A compelling story
- A vivid example
- A confident tone
- A clear conclusion

These are not inherently misleading. They become misleading when they replace substance.

When the story stands in for evidence.

When the example substitutes for pattern.

When confidence replaces support.

When the Structure Holds, but the Aim Shifts

An argument can be structurally sound and still be used to persuade selectively. The premises may be true. The reasoning may follow. But the choice of what to include can guide the conclusion.

You present one side clearly.

You omit what complicates it.

You lead the listener toward a particular outcome.

The argument works. But it doesn't tell the whole story.

The Role of the Listener

Persuasion is not just the responsibility of the speaker. It relies on the listener as well.

If you accept what sounds good without examination, persuasion becomes easier.

If you ask questions–if you apply the checklist from the previous chapter, you introduce resistance. Not opposition. Evaluation. And evaluation changes the dynamic.

Truth Under Pressure

In real-world situations, the pressure to persuade is strong.

A presentation.

A proposal.

A classroom.

A conversation where the outcome matters.

You are expected to be clear, confident, and convincing. But clarity can hide complexity. Confidence can obscure uncertainty.

So the question becomes:

How do you remain persuasive without losing accuracy?

Holding the Line

It's possible. But it requires intention.

You do three things:

1. Represent the idea fully

Not just the parts that support your case.

2. Acknowledge uncertainty

Not as weakness, but as reality.

3. Separate explanation from advocacy

Make it clear when you are describing and when you are arguing. This doesn't weaken your position. It strengthens your credibility.

When Persuasion Goes Wrong

The problem isn't persuasion itself.

It's when persuasion becomes detached from truth.

When the goal shifts entirely:

- Not to explain, but to convince
- Not to examine, but to win
- Not to understand, but to influence

At that point, reasoning becomes a tool for an outcome rather than a process for discovery. And once that shift happens, it's difficult to reverse.

Back to the Workshop

In the workshop, this is the difference between building something that works and building something that looks like it works.

The second may pass inspection at a glance. It may impress. It may hold for a moment. But under real use, the weaknesses appear. Because the goal wasn't durability. It was appearance.

What Comes Next

We've now moved from how thinking works to how it is used.

The final chapters turn inward again. Not to the mechanics, but to the mindset required to use them well. Because tools and processes are only part of the picture.

The rest is disposition.

How willing you are to question your own thinking.

How comfortable you are with uncertainty.

How ready you are to revise.

In the next chapter, we look at one of the most important, and most difficult of these:

Changing your mind.

For now, remember this:

Persuasion asks for agreement. Truth asks for examination. And the difference between the two is where thinking either strengthens or begins to drift.

Chapter Twenty One

The Discipline of Changing Your Mind

There is a sentence that sounds simple and feels expensive:

"I was wrong."

Not mistaken in a minor detail. Not slightly off. Wrong.

It is a small admission with a large cost. It asks you to set aside certainty, to loosen your grip on an idea that felt solid, and to replace it with something less familiar.

Most people avoid it. Not because they lack intelligence. Because they have identity.

Why Changing Your Mind Is Difficult

Ideas don't remain abstract for long.

> You express them.
>
> You defend them.
>
> You build arguments around them.

Over time, they become attached to you. They are no longer just thoughts. They are positions. And once a position is established, changing it feels like retreat.

It feels like losing ground. So the mind does what it does best.

> It explains.
>
> It defends.
>
> It finds reasons to stay where it is.

Consistency vs Accuracy

We value consistency. We expect people to hold their views, to stand by what they've said, to maintain a stable position over time.

Consistency signals reliability. But consistency and accuracy are not the same.

You can be consistently wrong. You can be accurately inconsistent. The goal of thinking is not to remain unchanged. It is to become more correct over time.

The Cost of Being Right

There is a quiet reward attached to being right.

It reinforces confidence.

It confirms judgment.

It signals competence.

But there is also a hidden cost. If being right becomes the goal, changing your mind becomes a threat.

New information is resisted.

Contradictions are minimized.

Alternatives are dismissed.

The workshop shifts from construction to preservation. And preservation, while comfortable, limits improvement.

The Role of the Inspector

The Inspector is designed to question ideas. But it often arrives late–after the idea has been accepted, defended, and integrated into your thinking.

At that point, questioning feels disruptive. So instead of evaluating, the Inspector is redirected.

It begins to justify.

It builds arguments that support the existing view.

It strengthens what is already in place.

This is not inspection. It's reinforcement.

Separating Ideas from Identity

The turning point comes when you separate the idea from yourself.An idea is something you have. It is not something you are.

Once that distinction is clear, something shifts.

You can examine the idea without feeling personally challenged.

You can revise it without feeling diminished. You can say, "This doesn't hold," without hearing, "You don't hold."

The Signal to Reconsider

You don't need to question everything all the time. But there are moments when reconsideration is warranted.

- When new information contradicts your conclusion
- When your reasoning relies on assumptions you haven't tested
- When the argument becomes harder to defend than to revise
- When you find yourself explaining rather than examining

These are not signs of failure. They are signals.

A Practical Approach

Changing your mind does not require a dramatic shift. It can be incremental. You don't need to move from certainty to the opposite position. You can move from certainty to less certainty.

From "This is true" to "This seems likely" to "I may need to reconsider this."

This preserves flexibility. And flexibility is what allows thinking to improve.

The Value of Revision

Every time you revise an idea, you strengthen your thinking. Not because the new idea is perfect. But because the process is active.

You are not holding a position.

You are working on it.

This is what distinguishes thinking from belief. Belief is held.

Thinking is adjusted.

A Familiar Moment

You encounter an argument that challenges your view.

At first, you resist. It doesn't feel right. It conflicts with what you know. Then something happens.

A detail.

A question.

A piece of evidence.

And the structure shifts.

Not completely. Just enough to notice. That moment, before you decide what to do with it–is the point of discipline.

Do you defend? Or, do you examine?

What It Looks Like in Practice

Changing your mind rarely looks dramatic.

It looks like:

- Adjusting a conclusion
- Refining an argument
- Acknowledging uncertainty
- Updating a position quietly

It may not be visible to others. But it is significant.

Because it reflects control over your thinking rather than attachment to it.

Back to the Workshop

In the workshop, this is the moment when you realize something doesn't fit.

A joint is slightly off. A measurement is just enough to matter.

You can force it. Or you can take it apart and rebuild.

One is faster. The other is better.

What Comes Next

We've now moved through the process of thinking–from generation to bias, from reasoning to revision.

The final step is broader. Not how you think alone, but how thinking functions in a larger environment.

Teams. Classrooms. Organizations.

Because thinking does not happen in isolation. It is shaped by the people and systems around it.

In the final chapter, we look at how to build environments where good thinking is not the exception–but the expectation.

For now, remember this:

Changing your mind is not a loss of ground.

It is the work of thinking done properly.

Chapter Twenty Two

Building a Thinking Culture

It's one thing to run a good workshop.

It's another to walk into a room where everyone is building that way.

Most thinking doesn't happen in isolation. It happens in classrooms, meetings, conversations, organizations–places where ideas are exchanged, challenged, reinforced, and sometimes quietly ignored. And in those places, something larger takes shape:

A thinking culture. Not what people say they value.
What they actually reward, tolerate, and repeat.

The Default Setting

Left alone, most groups drift toward the same pattern.

- The loudest voice carries weight
- The first idea becomes the working idea
- Agreement is mistaken for clarity
- Confidence is mistaken for correctness

The Shortcutter thrives here.

It moves quickly.

It simplifies.

It produces decisions.

And because the process feels efficient, it becomes the norm. Until the results begin to show the cost.

What a Thinking Culture Is

A thinking culture is not a set of rules.

It's a set of habits–shared expectations about how ideas are treated.

In a strong thinking culture:

- Ideas are examined, not just accepted
- Questions are expected, not avoided
- Revision is normal, not embarrassing
- Uncertainty is acknowledged, not hidden

It's not slower. It's more deliberate.

The Role of Leadership

Whether in a classroom or a boardroom, the tone is set early. What gets rewarded gets repeated.

If quick answers are praised, speed becomes the priority. If confident statements go unchallenged, confidence becomes currency.

But if thoughtful questioning is valued–if someone says, "Let's take a closer look at that, and that moment is respected, something shifts.

The Inspector is given permission to do its job. And once that permission exists, others begin to follow.

Normalizing the Pause

One of the simplest ways to change a thinking culture is to normalize the pause.

Not silence. Not hesitation. A brief moment where ideas are examined before being accepted.

It can be as simple as:

- "What supports that?"
- "What might we be missing?"
- "Is there another way to see this?"

These questions don't slow things down dramatically. They change the rhythm. From immediate acceptance to considered response.

Separating Ideas from People

In weak thinking cultures, ideas and identity become entangled.

A challenge to the idea feels like a challenge to the person.

So ideas are defended. Positions harden. Conversations narrow.

In a strong thinking culture, the separation is clear:

- The idea is examined
- The person is respected

This allows disagreement without conflict. And disagreement, when handled well, improves thinking.

Making Revision Visible

Changing your mind quietly is valuable. Making revision visible is transformative.

When someone says:

"I thought this was right, but I've reconsidered," it does two things.

It improves the idea. And it signals that revision is acceptable.

Over time, this changes the environment. People become less defensive. More open. More willing to adjust.

The Danger of Performance Thinking

In many settings, thinking becomes performance.

The goal shifts:

- To appear knowledgeable
- To present complete answers
- To avoid uncertainty

The Inventor becomes cautious. The Inspector becomes selective. And the Shortcutter fills the gap–offering quick, confident conclusions that look good but may not hold.

The result is polished thinking. Not necessarily good thinking.

Creating Space for Process

A thinking culture values process, not just outcomes.

It asks:

- How did we arrive at this?
- What assumptions shaped this decision?
- What alternatives were considered?

These questions don't undermine the result. They strengthen it. Because a good outcome reached by weak reasoning is fragile.

A good outcome reached by strong reasoning is repeatable.

A Practical Shift

You don't need to redesign the entire system. Small changes matter.

- Ask one more question before agreeing
- Invite one alternative before deciding
- Acknowledge one uncertainty before concluding

These are not dramatic. But they accumulate. And over time, they change how thinking happens.

A Familiar Environment

Think of a place where ideas are shared freely.

Where questions are welcomed.

Where disagreement is thoughtful, not personal.

Where people revise without hesitation.

That environment didn't happen by accident. It was built. One interaction at a time.

Back to the Workshop

In the workshop, culture shows up in how the work is treated.

Do people check each other's measurements?

Do they question assumptions?

Do they take the time to test what's been built?

Or do they move quickly, trusting that it will hold?

The difference isn't in the tools. It's in the expectations.

Closing the Loop

We began with a simple idea:

Thinking is not a single act. It's a process. Ideas are generated.

They are shaped by bias.

They are tested through reasoning.

They are revised.

That process can happen accidentally.

Or it can happen deliberately.

Individually–or collectively.

Final Thought

You don't control every idea that appears.

You don't eliminate bias.

You don't guarantee perfect reasoning.

But you can shape the conditions.

In your own thinking.

In your conversations.

In the environments you help create.

And in those conditions, something changes.

The first idea isn't the final one.

The loudest voice isn't the deciding one.

The most confident answer isn't the accepted one.

Instead, thinking becomes what it was always meant to be:

Not a performance. Not a defense. But a process. One that, with a little attention and a bit of discipline, gets better over time.

Epilogue

Leave the Light On

Workshops have a rhythm.

They open.

They fill with activity.

They quiet down.

At some point, the tools are set aside, the dust settles, and the door is pulled closed. Almost.

Almost.

Because a good workshop is never entirely shut. There's always a light left on somewhere in the back.

What You Take With You

> You won't remember every bias.
>
> You won't name every fallacy mid-conversation.
>
> You won't run a perfect thinking loop every time you face a decision.

That was never the point. The point was simpler.

> To notice.
>
> To recognize when an idea arrives too easily.
>
> To pause when something feels certain without effort.
>
> To ask a question before accepting an answer.

Not always. But more often than before.

The Work That Continues

Thinking does not finish. There is no final version.

No complete understanding that stays complete.

Ideas shift. Information changes. Assumptions reveal themselves, usually later than you'd prefer. So the work continues.

Not as a burden. As maintenance.

> A joint tightened here.
>
> A measurement checked there.
>
> A piece taken apart and rebuilt when it no longer fits.

The Value of Imperfection

You will still have bad ideas.

> Some will be obvious in hindsight.
>
> Some will take longer to reveal themselves.
>
> A few will linger longer than they should.

That's fine. The goal was never perfection. It was awareness. Because an imperfect process that notices its own flaws is stronger than a confident one that never looks.

A Different Kind of Confidence

There is a kind of confidence that comes from being certain. And another that comes from being willing to examine that certainty.

The first is louder. The second is steadier.

One defends. The other adjusts.

If you've gained anything from this, it's not a set of answers. It's a different relationship to your own thinking.

The Workshop Remains

The Inventor is still there, generating, connecting, wandering into ideas that may or may not be useful.

The Shortcutter is still there, moving quickly, simplifying, offering answers that feel right.

The Inspector is still there, waiting, as always, for a moment to step in and ask a better question.

They haven't changed. You have.

You know their voices now.

You recognize their timing.

You see where they help–and where they get in the way.

One Last Habit

If there is one habit worth carrying forward, it is this:

When something feels obvious, look at it again.

Not with suspicion. With attention. Because obvious ideas are often where thinking stops. And just beyond them is where it starts again.

Closing the Door *(But Not Quite)*

At the end of the day, the workshop quiets.

The tools are where you left them. The work is where you stopped.

But the light stays on. Not for what you've already built.

For what you haven't considered yet.

Final Line

You don't need to think perfectly.

You just need to keep thinking–carefully enough to notice, and honestly enough to adjust when the work calls for it.

Bibliography

Ariely, D. (2008). *Predictably irrational: The hidden forces that shape our decisions.* HarperCollins.

Catmull, E. (2014). *Creativity, Inc.: Overcoming the unseen forces that stand in the way of true inspiration.* Random House.

Chatfield, T. (2018). *Critical thinking: Your guide to effective argument, successful analysis and independent study.* SAGE Publications.

de Bono, E. (1970). *Lateral thinking: Creativity step by step.* Harper & Row.

de Bono, E. (1985). *Six thinking hats.* Little, Brown and Company.

Damer, T. E. (2013). *Attacking faulty reasoning: A practical guide to fallacy-free arguments (7th ed.).* Wadsworth.

Dobelli, R. (2013). *The art of thinking clearly.* Harper.

Donnelly, M. (2026). *Neuroscience for Business. Same Brain. New Toys: Why Business Keeps Forgetting How Humans Work (Graybeard Lectures).* RPSS Publishing

Gladwell, M. (2005). *Blink: The power of thinking without thinking.* Little, Brown and Company.

Kahneman, D. (2011). *Thinking, fast and slow.* Farrar, Straus and Giroux.

Kleon, A. (2014). *Show your work!: 10 ways to share your creativity and get discovered.* Workman Publishing.

Konnikova, M. (2013). *Mastermind: How to think like Sherlock Holmes.* Viking.

Pressfield, S. (2002). *The war of art: Break through the blocks and win your inner creative battles.* Black Irish Entertainment.

Rosling, H., Rosling Rönnlund, A., & Rosling, O. (2018). *Factfulness: Ten reasons we're wrong about the worldand why things are better than you think.* Flatiron Books.

Sagan, C. (1996). *The demon-haunted world: Science as a candle in the dark.* Random House.

Thouless, R. H. (1930). *Straight and crooked thinking.* Kegan Paul, Trench, Trubner & Co.

Warburton, N. (2000). *Thinking from A to Z (2nd ed.).* Routledge.

Weston, A. (2018). *A rulebook for arguments (5th ed.).* Hackett Publishing.

Almossawi, A. (2014). *An illustrated book of bad arguments.* The Experiment.

Syed, M. (2015). *Black box thinking: Why most people never learn from their mistakes–but some do.* Portfolio Penguin.

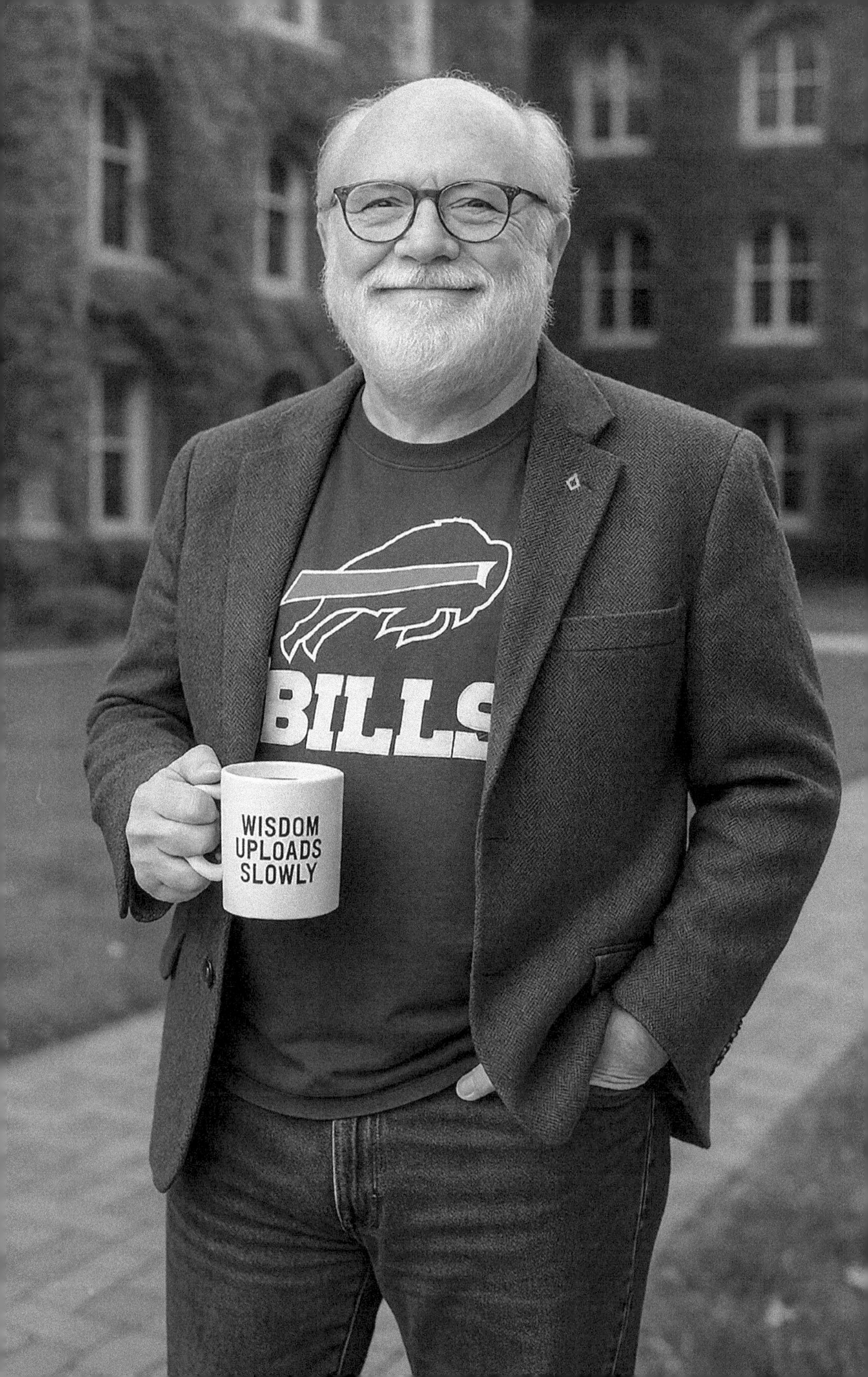
BILLS
WISDOM
UPLOADS
SLOWLY

About the Author

Mark Donnelly, PhD, is the graybeard lecturer who turned a squeaky whiteboard and a tie-dye shirt into a teaching philosophy. A marketing professor, brand consultant, author of 60+ books, historian, photographer, and creative instigator, he's spent decades making complex ideas feel simple – and making students wonder if it's all that coffee he drinks, or is he naturally this intense.

Dr. Donnelly built his reputation the old-fashioned way: by simplifying the truth. Not the buzzword-stuffed, corporate-approved version, but the real, human kind you only learn after watching trends rise, fall, and come back wearing different shoes.

Along with over 30 years in academia, he's wandered through newspapers, publishing, consulting, community work, and advertising, – collecting stories, experience, and more old books than any one man needs. Today, his whiteboard scribbles still inspire everyone from Master classes to CEOs, finally captured in print before the janitor could erase them.

Ask him what he truly is and he'll shrug:

> "A teacher at heart.
> A storyteller by accident.
> A graybeard by mileage."

He lives and creates in Buffalo, New York, with his bride Princess Laura and an ever-expanding pile of notebooks and half-finished ideas. His lifelong guiding principle remains simple:

Make a difference.

This book is his latest attempt to do exactly that.

Other Timeless Books in the Graybeard Lectures Series:

Each stands alone.

Together, they form a unique, common sense curriculum.

Graybeard Lectures: Marketing

Drawn from smudged whiteboards and lived experience, This book cuts through buzzwords and trends to reveal how branding, storytelling, word of mouth, and purpose actually work–by understanding humans first. Warm, humorous, and practical, it's a guide for anyone who wants marketing that makes sense and lasts.

Graybeard Lectures: Advertising

Advertising doesn't fail because people stopped paying attention. It fails because it forgets how attention works.

This book explores why the most effective advertising aligns with human instincts rather than fighting them. It examines timing, context, repetition, and emotional truth without chasing trends or tactics.

Graybeard Lectures: Market Research

Listening Past The Numbers is a clear-eyed look at why market research often delivers confidence instead of understanding. It challenges the misuse of data, dashboards, and statistics, arguing for research grounded in human behavior, context, and judgment. Rather than offering tools, the book offers a wiser way to think, listen, and decide when the numbers start acting certain.

Graybeard Lectures: Business Leadership

This is a clear-eyed guide for leaders and organizations overwhelmed by activity but starved for progress. With calm wit and long-earned perspective, it cuts through business noise to focus on what endures: human behavior, honest systems, and decisions that hold up over time.

www.ingramcontent.com/pod-product-compliance
Lightning Source LLC
LaVergne TN
LVHW052338100826
845147LV00020B/1101

* 9 7 8 1 9 5 6 6 8 8 7 4 0 *